CAPRICIOUS GLOBAL EDUCATION FOR PEACE (for All) & PROGRESSIVE SUSTAINABLE DEVELOPMENT WORLD:

MIND SHIFT BEYOND THE 21st CENTURY, WITH EPILOGUE

CAPRICIOUS GLOBAL EDUCATION FOR PEACE (for All) & PROGRESSIVE SUSTAINABLE DEVELOPMENT WORLD:

MIND SHIFT BEYOND THE 21st CENTURY, WITH EPILOGUE

O. P. GOYAL

GYAN

Published by

GYAN

Gyan Publishing House
5, Ansari Road
Daryaganj, New Delhi-110002
Phone: 011-47034999, 9811692060
E-mail: books@gyanbooks.com

Distribution Network
gyanbooks.com
India, USA, Canada, UK, Australia, France

ISBN: 978-93-7097-040-3 (PB)
First Published, 2025

Printed at: Gyan Press, Delhi.

CAPRICIOUS GLOBAL EDUCATION FOR PEACE (for All) & PROGRESSIVE SUSTAINABLE DEVELOPMENT WORLD: MIND SHIFT BEYOND THE 21st CENTURY, WITH EPILOGUE

Author : O. P. GOYAL

Contents

The Alone Source of Peace and Progressive Sustainable World is "Capricious Global Education" to its human families. And, Global education is hardly edifying without the provision for 'Ethics', 'Human Values', 'Code of Conduct' and 'Character'.

With profound regards to the human families whose peace is the foundation of the future of mankind.

Peace & Progressive Sustainable World would be the awakend divine before whom all heads bend, except those of the insane.

AUSPICATE

Why and what for this Study? It is primarily for the common men and women of this World. It is just to make them understand as to where they are living? What are their geopolitical boundaries? Who are their neighbours? What are the dominant features of their current social and economic environment? What kind of institutional setup they are faced within their day-to-day life? This aside, this endeavour intends to accomplish one more critical purpose, namely, creating awareness among the members of this world about the probable challenges likely to be faced by them in the couple of decades/centuries ahead of them. And, we propose to close this Study by suggesting the way out for challenges of which some are unhypothetical, but others are really hypothetical.

ACKNOWLEDGEMENTS

This Study owes its depth and accuracy to the invaluable assistance of META AI, which provided essential information and statistics. I extend my gratefulness to this remarkable tool. Additionally, I am deeply indebted to my Beloved Family whose multifaceted support was instrumental in completing this rather gigantic task. I once again express my deepest gratitude to all of them.

CHAPTER – 1

THE EARTH: ITS COUNTRIES AND THEIR EXPLICATIONS AND PERSPICUITIES

The Surface Area of Earth is 197 million square miles (510 million square kilometres). And, of this, around 57 million square miles (148 square kilometres) or 29 percent is land and remaining 140 million square miles (362 square kilometres) or 71 percent is covered by water[1]. This total surface area can also be called "**World**".

As to the question: How many countries are there in the world? This question appears to be simple but the answer is surprisingly quite complex as there is no universal agreement on the total; as per different sources, the total number of countries on Earth ranges anywhere between 193 to 237. As per US Intelligence Agency Listing the total number too is 237. Well, it is ultimate as there are lot of disputed zones and nations that hold either full or partial sovereignty around the world.

Without involving ourselves in any kind of controversy let us accept the United Nation's version which is regarded today as the **de facto** authority on '**Nationhood**'. So according to United Nations there are 195 recognised countries in the world; 193 of these are **Member States** and two are **Non-Member Observers States-** Holy See/ Vatican City and Palestine. These two countries are self-ruling countries but are not considered as full-fledged countries[2].

A against the UN's list, **Britannica's** list depicts the total number of countries as 196 – Vatican City, Taiwan and Kosovo are treated as full-fledged countries. Wikipedia's list of sovereign states includes: UN's list of 193 countries and Two Observer States; and, 11 other sovereign states for a total of 206. Keeping in view the focus of this study on Capricious Global Education and its role in attaining progressive sustainable world with peace for all during the time frame beyond 21st Century, we accept the UN version, as it would not matter if the total number of countries slightly varies. 193 countries of the world are classified into three broad categories on the basis of their economic growth[3] by United Nations in 1960, namely, Developed or Advanced Countries, Developing Countries and Least Developed Countries.

Developed Countries

As per Wikipedia, a developed country or an advanced country is a sovereign state that has a high quality of life, developed economy and advanced technological infrastructure analogous to other less industrialised nations. And, as per UN, developed countries (also known as high income countries) are those which have high standard of living, strong economies and advanced infrastructure. As of now these countries possess the undermentioned three basic features:

(i) High income which means that the per capita GNI[4] is above $12,746;

(ii) Human Development Index (HDI) is either High or Very High;[5] and,

(iii) Institutional Framework is quite strong.

These countries normally have such key indicators as : High per capita GDP, lower unemployment rate (<5%), lower rate of inflation (<3%), strong currency, significant foreign exchange reserves, multiple industrial base, high value of exports, favourable environments for businesses, lower ratio of debt to GDP and a highly strong institutional framework[6]. Not only this, these countries are also backed by strong structural features like: developed transportation, energy and communication levels, advanced technology and innovations, highly skilled workforce, efficient financial systems, effective governance and regulatory framework, strong research and development, encouragement to entrepreneurships and start-ups and strategic trade agreements and partnerships. And, so long as these countries are able to sustain the present level of education of human capital, innovation and R&D efforts coupled with natural resources, institutional and macroeconomic stability, strategic location, trade and government policies and regulations, cultural and social factors and global connectivity, they would continue to maintain their status as developed countries. The complete list of these countries can be viewed in Annexure 1:1 appended at the end of this Chapter. Accordingly, there are **39 developed countries** in the world.[7]

Developing Countries[8]

Developing countries are also known as 'Lower Income' or 'Middle Income' countries as per World Bank. The Bank placed these in two sub-categories, namely, one, those where we find lower-middle-economies i.e., where the GNI per capita ranges between $ 1026 - $ 4035; and, two, those where we find 'upper-middle-income' economies i.e., where GNI per capita varies between $4036 - $12475.[9] In upper-middle-income countries the potential for economic growth is, however, found 'high'. This high potential is adjudged by the growth rate of GDP/ GNI, increase in productivity, higher income and rise in standards of living, increased job opportunities and low unemployment rates, increased investment in infrastructure and better education and health care and growing international trade aside enhanced economic stability. The growth in these countries is again facilitated by multiple factors, such as, innovations and technological advancements, investments in capital expenditure, human capital – education and skills, institutional framework, effective governance and regulations, international trade agreements, availability and management of natural resources, fiscal and monetary policies.

However, the pattern of growth in these countries may depict variety of patterns. It could be **sustained growth** (long term increase in economic output), **rapid growth** (fast increase in economic output often driven by technological advancements or investment), **stagnant growth** (slow or no increase in economic output) and **negative growth** (contraction in economic output). Some of the unhealthy patterns might be caused due to the number of challenges which these countries may face from time to time. The major challenges include: inflation, income inequalities, political instability, corruption, environmental degradation, debt accumulation and global economic shocks.The lists of these countries are included in Annexure 1.2 and 1.3 presented towards the close of this Chapter. According to these lists, the number of upper-middle-income and lower-middle-income countries stood at 36 and 40, respectively.

Least Developed Countries

On the basis of low per capita GNI (<=$1025), weak health, education and literacy ratio of humans, and economic vulnerability (as adjudged on the basis of instability in agricultural production, concentration of exports in merchandise, economic importance of non-traditional activities, handicap of economic smallness and displacement of population due to national disasters, the number of LDC, stood at 46 as per UN and

World Bank[10]. This list is presented in Annexure 1.4 at the end of this Chapter. In the context of definition of LDCs, it may be pertinent, as well of interest, to mention that this list of LDCs is reviewed every three years by a Committee for Development Policy (CDP), a group of independent experts that reports to the Economic and Social Council (ECOSOC) of the United Nations[11].

Common characteristics which are often found in LDCs, due to their histories and/or geographies are: lower levels of access to safe drinking water, sanitation and hygiene, energy, poverty, higher levels of pollutions, higher proportions of people with tropical and infectious diseases, more road traffic accidents and generally poorer quality of infrastructure. In addition, these countries generally have higher levels of unemployment, widespread poverty, hunger, child labour, malnutrition, homelessness, substance abuse, prostitution, over population, civil disorder, a large informal economy, high crime rates, low education levels, economic inequalities, corruption at all government levels, political instability and lack of rule of law, school desertion, etc. These countries are also characterized by low access to health care causing lower life expectancies, child and maternal mortality, lower climate resistance and lower and median ages.

*****

ENDNOTES

1. According to NOAA – National Oceanic & Atmospheric Administration – it was first estimated by Greek Philosopher 'Aristotle', and later improved by Greek Polymath Eratosthenes, mathematically, around 250 B.C.
2. U.N. does not consider today Taiwan as a separate country, which it used to be between 1945 and 1971. Now Taiwan is considered as a territory of mainland China. Likewise, up to 2020, Kosovo was considered as a separate country but it is now regarded as a part of Serbia.
3. Economic Development or economic growth refers to the increase in production of goods and services in an economy overtime – which is measured as percentage change in Gross Domestic Product (GDP) or Gross National Product (GNP) or Net Domestic Product (NDP).
4. GNI means Gross National Income which measures the total income earned by a country's citizens regardless of location. So, GNI is GNP+ income from foreign investments – income paid to foreigners. Thus, it reflects the country's total income including international flaws.
5. HDI measures the quality of life, education and economic standards in a country. It is computed based on three dimensions: a long and healthy life, knowledge and decent living standards. HDI scores range from 0 to 1, with scores above

0.800 considered Very High, 0.700 – 0.799 High and 0.550 – 0.699 Medium and below 0.550 Low. Some examples of countries having very high HDI are: Norway, Iceland, Hongkong, Denmark, Sweden, Ireland, Germany, Singapore, Netherland and Australia. These countries have low poverty rates, high standards of living, advanced infrastructure, high level of economic diversification and strong education and health care systems.

6. Couple of examples of Developed Countries include: United States, Germany, Japan, United Kingdom, Australia, Canada, Switzerland, Sweden, Singapore and South Korea. In the context it may be of interest to note that economics of China, India, Brazil, Russia, Indonesia, Turkey, Poland, Thailand, Vietnam and Malaysia are also emerging strong.
7. This list may not tally with the similar list brought out by IMF and OECD.
8. There are varied definitions of the phrase 'Developing Countries'. For example, as per Wikipedia a developing country is a sovereign state with a less developed industrial base and a lower Human Development Index (HDI). This definition, however, is not agreed upon universally as there is not found an agreement as to which countries fit this category. There is another school of thought according to which the phrases Low and Middle Income Country and Newly Emerging Economy can be used interchangeably.The World Bank has classified all the world's economies into 4 groups based on Per Capita Gross National Income, namely, High, Upper-Middle, Lower-Middle and Low-Income Countries
9. This is as per World Bank's definitions cited in footnote above.
10. In 2024.
11. It may be noted in this context that the criterion for this review have been again three: (i) GNI per capita – the threshold for inclusion is \$1088 or below and for graduation \$1306 or above; (ii) A Human Assets Index (HAI) comprising of two sub-indices: A health sub-index and an education sub-index. The Health sub-index has 3 indicators – the under 5 mortality rate, the maternal mortality ratio and prevalence of stunting. The Education sub-index has 3 indicators – lower secondary school completion rate, adult literacy rate and gender parity index for lower secondary school completion; (iii) An Economic and Environmental Vulnerability Index (EVI) which again consists of two sub-indices: Economic Vulnerability sub-index and an Environment Vulnerability sub-index. The Economic Vulnerability sub-index has 4 indicators – (a) share of agriculture, forestry and fishing in GDP; (b) remoteness and land lockedness; (c) merchandise export concentration; and (d) instability of exports of goods and services. The Environmental Vulnerability sub index has 4 indicators (a) share of population in low elevated coastal zones; (b) share of population living in drylands; (c) stability of agricultural production; and (d) victims of disasters.

    On the above basis no recommendations were made for inclusion at CDP's 2021 triennial review. The same happened as per the latest report 2024/33 (Supplement No. 13) submitted to the UN on its 26th Plenary Session held from March 4-8, 2024.

Annexure: 1.1

LIST OF DEVELOPED COUNTRIES

($ 12475 or more)

1. Norway ($70,590)	**HIGH INCOME COUNTRIES:**
2. Switzerland ($64,660)	1. Luxembourg ($105,934)
3. Iceland ($63,830)	2. Qatar ($69,962)
4. United States ($63,680)	3. Ireland ($68,310)
5. Denmark ($62,200)	4. United Arab Emirates ($67,140)
6. Australia ($61,940)	5. Brunei ($64,570)
7. Netherlands ($61,110)	6. Taiwan ($63,420)
8. Sweden ($60,440)	7. South Korea ($62,790)
9. Singapore ($59,660)	8. Portugal ($62,490)
10. Canada ($59,520)	9. Finland ($62,230)
11. Belgium ($58,610)	**OECD COUNTRIES:**
12. New Zealand ($58,390)	1. Estonia ($34,910)
13. Japan ($57,850)	2. Slovenia ($34,660)
14. United Kingdom ($57,630)	3. Czech Republic ($33,920)
15. Germany ($56,980)	4. Poland ($33,740)
16. France ($56,760)	5. Hungary ($32,810)
17. Italy ($55,930)	6. Turkey ($28,440)
18. Israel ($55,730)	7. Greece ($27,810)
19. Spain ($54,910)	8. Slovakia ($26,910)
20. Australia ($54,630)	9. Chile ($24,588)
	10. Mexico ($24,440)

Source: GNI figures are in US$, based on the year 2022 and the data is from the World Bank.

Annexure: 1.2

LIST OF UPPER MIDDLE-INCOME GROUP OF DEVELOPING COUNTRIES [$4036-$12,475]

(I) ASIA	(III) LATIN AMERICA
1. Malaysia	1. Chile
2. Thailand	2. Argentina
3. China	3. Uruguay
4. Turkey	4. Panama
5. South Korea	5. Costa Rica
6. Singapore	6. Colombia
7. Brunei	7. Brazil
8. Kazakhstan	8. Mayico
9. Azerbaijan	9. Venezula
10. Armenia	10. Ecvadar
(II) AFRICA	**(IV) EAST EUROPE & CENTRAL ASIA**
1. Botswana	1. Czech Republic
2. Mauritius	2. Estonia
3. Seychelles	3. Slovenia
4. Gabon	4. Lithuania
5. Cape Verde	5. Latvia
6. Namibia	6. Poland
	7. Hungary
	8. Croatia
	9 Romania
	10. Bulgaria

Source: World Bank 2022, IMF, UNDP and World Economic Outlook.

Annexure: 1.3

LIST OF LOWER MIDDLE-INCOME ECONOMIES ($1026-$4035)

(I) ASIA	**(III) LATIN AMERICA**
(1) Indonesia	(1) Brazil
(2) Phillipines	(2) Mexico
(3) Vietnam	(3) Colombia
(4) India	(4) Peru
(5) Pakistan	(5) Ecuador
(6) Bangladesh	(6) Dominican Republic
(7) Sri Lanka	(7) El Salvador
(8) Mongolia	(8) Guatemala
(9) Cambodia	(9) Honduras
(10) Laos	(10) Costa Rica
(II) AFRICA	**(IV) EASTERN EUROPE & CENTRAL ASIA**
(1) South Africa	(1) Bulgaria
(2) Morocco	(2) Romania
(3) Egypt	(3) Croatia
(4) Ghana	(4) Hungary
(5) Kenya	(5) Poland
(6) Nigeria	(6) Turkey
(7) Tanzania	(7) Ukraine
(8) Ethiopia	(8) Belarus
(9) Uganda	(9) Albania
(10) Rwanda	(10) Bosnia

Source: World Bank 2022, IMF, United Nations Development Programme (UNDP) and World Economic Outlook (WEO)

Annexure: 1.4

LIST OF LDCs AS PER UN OFFICE OF THE HIGH REPRESENTATIVE FOR LEAST DEVELOPED COUNTRIES, LANDLOCKED DEVELOPING COUNTRIES AND SMALL ISLAND DEVELOPING STATES (UN-OHRLLS) AND WORLD BANK (GROUPED BY REGION)* [BELOW $1025]

(I) AFRICA (33)

(1) Angola
(2) Benin
(3) Burkina Faso
(4) Burundi
(5) Central African Republic
(6) Chad
(7) Comoros
(8) Cote d'luaive
(9) Democratic Republic of the Congo
(10) Djibouti
(11) Equatorial Guinea
(12) Eritrea
(13) Ethiopia
(14) Gambia
(15) Guinea
(16) Guinea – Bissau
(17) Liberia
(18) Madagascar
(19) Malawi
(20) Mali
(21) Mauritania
(22) Mozambique
(23) Niger
(24) Rwanda
(25) Sao Tome & Principe
(26) Senegol
(27) Sierra – Leone
(28) Somalia
(29) South Dudan
(30) Sudan
(31) Tanzania
(32) Togo
(33) Uganda

(II) ASIA (9)

(1) Afghanistan
(2) Bangladesh
(3) Bhutan
(4) Cambodia
(5) Laos
(6) Myanmar
(7) Nepal
(8) Timor-Leste
(9) Yemen

(III) OCEANIA (4)

(1) Kiribati
(2) Samoa
(3) Soloman Islands
(4) Tuvalu

(IV) LATIN AMERICA AND THE CARRIBEAN (1)

(1) Haiti

* This list may change over time as countries graduate or meet the criteria.

CHAPTER - 2

EXTRINSIC DATA BANK

Our world is on Planet Earth and it is occupied by 195 countries, of which some are developed, and some others are developing and the rest least developed. But these facts alone does not allow us to justify the present study and its framework. Some other details of this Global World and these countries are needed further. About the Global World, picture in respect to its population, growth, per capita income, educational standards and technological developments would be of interest to peruse. Likewise, the identical details concerning different groups of countries would be of relevance. Among technological advancements, the growth of AI (Artificial Intelligence) and its major trends need to be highlighted along the perspectives and focus on future growth of AI. In the context, there is a widespread of the news that AI could be misused for causing international conflicts and its super-intelligence model may became instrumental for World War III. The current status of AI and international conflicts on the one hand, and that of accompanied variegated mal-practices, scams, frauds, corruptions, money laundering and competition and jealousy, on the other, requires to be explored before we proceed ahead.

Although "growth" in different countries of the world is taken care of by their Governments/political set up, even so, a set of institutions is found operative both at global and regional levels which intervenes in the process of growth *via* settling several issues/problems and financially aiding it. This set of institutions virtually functions under the broad directions/guidance of United Nations Organization. In view of this pivot role, an overview of the existing institutional set up both at Global and regional levels and their actual functioning would further be relevant and contextual. The subsequent paragraphs of this chapter cover this information as well.

1. WORLD's POPULATION[1]

The total population of the world is approximately 8.2 billion as on November 17, 2024 and it is projected to reach 9 billion by 2037 and 10 billion by 2060. Of this developed, developing and LDCs account for 1.7 billion (20.5%), 5.6 billion (68.3%) and 934 million (11.2%), respectively. Region wise Asia[2] accounts for the largest share with 4.8 billion people, followed by Africa[3] with 1.5 billion, Europe with 745 million and Latin America and the Caribbean with 663 million, Northern America with 385 million and Oceania with 46 million. It may be of interest that while the world's population will continue to grow, but at a slower rate than in the past. The annual growth rate has declined from 2.07% in 1970 to 0.87% in 2024, and is further expected to decrease to 0.47% by 2050.

2. GROWTH RATES: OVERALL PICTURE

The rates at which the different categories of the countries are growing differ significantly. Developed countries are growing at a slower rates viz-à-viz developing countries due to their already established economies. Thus in developed countries the average growth rate ranges between one to three percent per annum. In contrast to this, the average growth rates in developing countries range between four to seven percent per annum. The least developed countries, however, struggle to achieve a higher growth rate up to seven percent or more in order to eradicate poverty. Most of them, however, are not able to attain in actuality, though there are enough of opportunities to register a higher growth rate. For example, they can invest in human capital and education, adopt open ended trade policies to aid the trade and upgrade the productive capacities and take up structural transformations. But they fail in doing so on account of vulnerability to boom and bust cycles in commodity markets, limited access to medical health services and resources and high levels of poverty and inequality.

Region-wise picture in respect to growth rates is as thus: 4-6% growth rate in Asia and Oceania; 3-5% in Sub-Saharan Africa; at 2-4% in Latin America and the Caribbean.

3. OVERVIEW OF AVERAGE PER CAPITA INCOME (GNI/GDI) IN DEVELOPED, DEVELOPING AND LDCs BASED ON WORLD BANK[4]

The average GNI per capita for developed countries varies between

$45,000 and $ 55,000. An illustrative statistics is also given hereunder for most talked about developed countries:

1. United States: $ 69,862
2. Germany: $49,206
3. United Kingdom: $43,544
4. Japan: $43,474
5. Australia: $51,885
6. Canada: $52,263
7. France: $41,862
8. Italy: $34,704
9. Sweden: $53,764
10. Switzerland: $80,530

In contrast to the above, the average GNI per capita varied in the range of $3,000 and $10,000 in case of developing countries.[5] This being so in the case of following countries:

1. Brazil: $ 9,671
2. China: $ 10,260
3. India $ 2,134
4. Indonesia: $3,844
5. Mexico: $9,341
6. Russia: $11,216
7. South Africa: $6,401
8. Turkey: $10,541
9. Vietnam: $2,470
10. Egypt: $2,450

In so far as LDCs are concerned, the average GNI per capita varies in range of $400-$2000. The following 10 LDCs have the GNI per capita as thus:

1. Afghanistan: $ 694
2. Angola: $2,041
3. Bangladesh: $2,064
4. Burundi: $277
5. Cambodia: $1,440
6. Democratic Republic Congo: $444
7. Ethiopia: $844
8. Haiti: $784
9. Liberia: $351
10. Mozambique: $460

World's region-wise average GNI per capita has been:

1. Sub-Saharan Africa: $ 1,656
2. South Asia. $ 2,064
3. East Asia and Pacific: $ 10,342
4. Latin America & Caribbean: $ 9,341
5. Middle East & North Africa: $ 6,401

4. EDUCATIONAL STANDARDS[6]

The standards of education is quite high in developed countries and this fact is supported by both the broad and precise parameters like literacy rate (95% or higher), enrolment rates (90% or higher at primary and 85%

or higher in secondary level; it being 70% or higher in teritiary), and quality of education (as seen *via* high quality of teacher-training, emphasis on STEM education as well as by equipped schools.[7] It may be added that STEM fields play a critical role in innovation and technological advancements. Also, they constitute the core of economic growth and development, critical thinking and problem-solving skills, aside addressing global challenges like climate change, health care and energy.

In these countries the average years of schooling range between 16-18 years over and above the higher scores of Reading (500-600), Mathematics (500-600) and Science (500-600) in Programme for International Student Assessment (PISA). The Finland has ranked quite high in PISA and Singapore quite strong in emphasis on STEM and Canada in High quality of Teacher-training.

The comparative picture of developing and least developed countries in this respect is as found hereunder:

(i) **Developing Countries:** Literacy and Enrolment rates in these countries are found between 60-90% and enrolment between 70-90% (primary level), 40-70% (secondary level) and 20-40% (tertiary level), respectively. We observe variable quality of education depending upon teachers' training. In view of limited resources, the focus is on Basic Education. Average years of schooling range between 10-14 years and PISA scores for reading, maths and science are found varying between 400-500. Even so, there is an emphasis on improving the infrastructure for education in Brazil, on vocational training in China and on Digital Education in India.

(ii) **Least Developed Countries:** The Literacy Rate in LDCs vary between 40-60% and enrolment rates are 50-70% at primary level, 20-40% at secondary level and 10-20% in tertiary level. The quality of education is hindered due to inadequate resources and limited teacher-training. The focus of education therefore is found on Basis Literacy. Average years of schooling is 6-10 years and PISA scores varies between 300-400 in all the three areas, namely, Reading, Maths and Science. In general, the standard of education in LDCs is quite poor due to inadequate infrastructure, limited resources, poor teacher training facilities and the long-term challenges they are facing on almost every front. But then, they are taking initiatives to improve it *via* adoption programmes like UN Sustainable Development Goal 4 (SDG_{-4}). UNESCO's

Education for All (EFA), World Bank's Education Global Practice and Global Partnership for Education.

5. TECHNOLOGICAL GROWTH: MAJOR TRENDS HIGHLIGHTED INCLUDING THE ADVANCEMENTS IN AI

In developed countries like USA, Canada, UK, Germany, Australia, Japan, etc. we find high speed (80-90%) penetration of internet; adoption of smartphone by 70-80% population; $10 to 50 billion annual investment in AI in advanced research and development and in widespread use of AI in health care, finance, transportation and education. Resultantly the places like Silicon Valley, New York, London and Tokyo are emerging as Global Tech Hubs[8]. In contrast to above, in developing countries like China, India, Brazil, South Africa and Mexico and several others, the internet penetration is 30-70%; smartphone adoption is 30-60%; and, annual investment in AI is $1-10 Billion and this investment is in AI research and development and its growing applications in e-commerce, finance and health care. Consequently, Bangalore, Beijing, Sao Paulo and Nairobi have emerged as Tech Hubs representing this category of countries. The comparative position in LDCs (Afghanistan, Brunei, Mozambique and Seira-Leone) is however, not good. Internet penetration and adoption of smartphone is found only 10-30% and the annual investment is in AI between $10,000-$1 million in research, development and applications. So far, no place has been able to emerge as Tech Hub representing these countries.

GLOBAL TREND OBSERVED IN REGARD TO AI

The initiatives are being taken for the development of AI for social good by ITU (International Telecommunication Union), World Bank, UNCTAD (United Nations Conference on Trade & Development) and McKinsey Global Institute. These efforts are worth appreciating as the same are being done despite numerous challenges like digital divide, infrastructural limitations, talent shortages, data privacy concerns and regulatory frameworks.

PERSPECTIVES AND FOCUS OF FUTURE GROWTH OF AI

Next decades are going to witness significant growth of AI. The Global AI market is likely to jump from $190 billion in 2020 to $500 billion in 2025 and further to $15.7 Trillion in 2028. The percentage of AI adoption in varied businesses is going to touch 80% in 2025 from the low of 30% in 2020. The AI related job growth is forecasted to be 30% YoY basis between 2020-2025, and that of investment from mere $50 billion in 2020 to $150 billion in 2025. Also, there will be growth in AI powered services from 20% in 2020 to 40% in 2025.

The region wise focus areas of AI use are likely to be: Health care, Finance and Transportation in North America; Manufacturing, energy and education in Europe; e-commerce, finance and health care in Asia Pacific; agriculture, education and health care in Latin America; and Agriculture, Health care and finance in Africa. Sector-wise the status of AI use by 2025 is forecasted as thus: 30% medical diagnoses, 50% of trading decisions, 20% of transportation by autonomous vehicles and 30% conduct of courses in education.

6. MALPRACTICES, FRAUDS AND SCAMS

Another quite common feature of the working of our countries concerns with the malpractices, frauds and scams in day to day life. These are certainly not good, but then these constitute one of the hard realities of day. 'Malpractices' refer to professional or occupational misconduct, involving negligence, incompetence, unethical behaviour, breach of standards and harm/ injury to others. In other words, a malpractice is the failure of a professional or organization to meet the standards of care, ethics or laws governing their field, resulting in harm or damage to clients, customers or society. These could be intentional or unintentional. The negligence or mismanagement generally causes unintentional malpractices. Intentional deception or misrepresentation, false claims or promises to obtain benefit/ advantage, concealment of facts/ truth, harm or financial loss to victims or any act involving criminal intent could be phrased as 'frauds'. Deceptive schemes or tricks to obtain money or benefit, false promises/pretences/psychological, manipulation, harm/financial loss to victims, either offline or online are clubbed in phrase 'scams'.[9]

KEY DIFFERENCES

The major differences between, 'malpractices', 'frauds' and 'scams' revolve around their 'nature', 'scope' and 'intent'. In terms of nature, malpractices involve professional misconduct, while frauds and scams involve deception. Scope-wise, malpractices often affect specific clients or customers, while frauds and scams can affect larger groups of people or society as a whole. Intentwise, malpractices could be both intentional and unintentional, frauds and scams are always intentional. There can be overlapping also. Malpractices can lead to frauds or scams and frauds and scams can involve malpractices. In so far as legal consequences are concerned; malpractices may need for their ratification, regulatory action, and/ or fines or lawsuits or any other combination. The frauds and scams both need criminal charges, fines and/or imprisonment.

LITTLE BIT OF DETAILS

It is even puzzling to attempt to count and describe the macro and micro details of malpractices. Just for interest we can describe the nature and types of financial frauds/ scams inclusive of those carried out *via* AI.

FINANCIAL FRAUDS/ SCAMS

1. **Ponzi Schemes:** Launching of fake investment opportunities, promising unusuably high returns. These are fraudulent investment plans wherein no money is invested at all! Instead, every new investment is used to pay off earlier investors.
2. **Pyramid Schemes:** Schemes which promise consumers or investors large profits based primarily on recruiting others to join their programmes not based on profits from any real investment or real sale of goods to the public. Some schemes may purport to sell a product, but they simply use the product to hide their pyramid structure.
3. **Identity Fraud:** Someone impersonates you and uses your personal information to steal money. These kinds of frauds are quite common. Internet fraudsters give instructions for fraudulent money transfer.
4. **Phishing Scams:** Internet Banking clients receive e-mails which are tricky asking them to give account login and password and personal details to website which look like their legitimate Bank. These details are then exploited to steal money from the concerned account.
5. **Advance Fee Scams:** These scams are usually perpetrated through a letter, e-mail or phone call offering a large sum of money if you can help someone transfer millions of rupees or other currency out of the country. To initiate the transactions, you are asked to send details of your bank account and an administration fee.
6. **Card Frauds:** (a) Starts with the theft of your bank card; stolen or lost cards remain usable. Thief make unauthorised purchases with the card until you notify your Bank. (b) Skimming: This

involves stealing information off a credit card during a legitimate transaction. Fraudsters swipe the card through an electronic device known as a "wedge" or "skimming device" which records all information contained on the magnetic strip. The information so stolen is used for online purchases. (c) Counterfeit Cards: The fraudsters make FAKE CARDS or sell the card information stolen as described above. The victim rarely knows as he still has the real card in his possession.

7. **Fake Prizes:** A perpetrator claims that you have won a non-existent prize. And you are asked to send a cheque to pay the taxes, or your credit card details or your account number to pay for shipping and handling charges to send you the non-existent prize.

8. **Inheritance Scams:** Receiving an e-mail from an 'Estate Locator' or 'Research Specialist' purporting an unclaimed inheritance or refund. You are lured into sending a fee to receive information about how to obtain the purported asset.

9. **Wills and Legacies:** A letter or e-mail is sent to you claiming that someone has died or had mentioned your name in his will. Usually, the scammer will claim to be the deceased's legal advisor and may claim an advance fee.

10. **Binary Options Scams: These cover fraudulent trading platforms.**

    (a) Online Scams

    - **(i) Romance Scams:** Fake online relationships seeking financial gains.
    - **(ii) Lottery and Prize scams:** Fake notifications of winning large sums.
    - **(iii) Online Auction Scams:** Fake product sales or bidding.
    - **(iv) Investment Scams:** Fake investment opportunities in crypto-currencies, real estate, etc.
    - **(v) CEO E-mails Scams:** Impersonating executives to strick employees into transferring funds.

    (b) PHONE & SMS SCAMS

    - **(i) Robocall Scams:** Automated calls promoting fake services or products.
    - **(ii) SMS Phishing (Smishing):** Text messages seeking sensitive information.

(iii) **On-Ring Scams:** Calling and hanging up to encourage call-back.

(c) **Travel and Holiday Scams:**

(i) **Fake Travel Agencies:** Selling non-existent packages.

(ii) **Hotel Reservation Scams:** Fake booking websites.

(iii) **Timeshare Scams:** Fraudulent property sales.

(d) **Health and Medical Scams**

(i) **Fake Online Pharmacies:** Selling counterfeit or harmful medicines.

(ii) **Weight Loss Scams:** Promoting ineffective or harmful products.

(iii) **Medical Billing Scams:** Fake medical billing services.

(e) **Govt. and Tax Scams**

(i) **IRS Scams:** Impersonating tax authorities to demand payment.

(ii) **Social Security Scams:** Phishing for sensitive information.

(iii) **Grant Scams:** Fake Government grants and loans.

(f) **Other Notable Scams**

(i) **Cryptocurrency Scams:** Fake ICOs, exchanges or wallets.

(ii) **Charity Scams:** Fake charitable organizations.

(iii) **Tech Support Scams:** Fake technical support services.

On the above basis, it is evident that in almost every field frauds/ scams are found. Hence, we need to be vigilant or report suspicious activities. Aside local and country-wise Websites/ Telephone numbers on which such activities can be reported, there are Global Hotlines also, such as, (i) US: Federal Trade Commission (FTC)– 1–877–FTC–HELP [1-877-382-4357]; (ii) UK Action 03001232040; (iii) Australia – Australian Competition and Consumer Commission (Accc) 1300302502

SUPPORTIVE STATISTICS/INFORMATION

Not the latest, yet we can have an idea about the volume of malpractices/ frauds/ scams that are being done at global and regional levels, and also in developed, developing and the least developed countries.

GLOBAL LEVEL SCENARIO

The global level scenario of malpractices, frauds and scams is as thus:

(i) **Malpractices:** 34% of the patients reported experiencing medical malpractices as per WHO 2019; 25% of professionals face malpractices lawsuits (Insurance Journal, 2020); and, $300 billion is the annual cost of medical malpractices in US alone (Journal of Patient Safety, 2019).

(ii) **Frauds:** Total number of fraud cases reported, and the victims were 3.5 million and 500 million, respectively as per ACFE 2020; and the annual cost of these frauds was $5.1 trillion; these apart, 27% of organizations experienced fraud (PwC, 2020).

(iii) **Corruption:** The total number of victims of corruption cases and the volume of corruption had been 1 billion and $2.6 Trillion, respectively, as per WHO 2020.

(iv) **Cybercrimes:** The total number of victims and the amount involved in cybercrimes had been 300 million and $600 billion, respectively, as per Cyber Security Ventures 2020; out of these only 1.8 million reported their cases.

(v) **Money Laundering:** As per UNODC, 2020, the money laundering had been equivalent to $ 1.6 Trillion.

(vi) **Scams:** The total number of cases reported and the total number of victims had been 1.2 million and 200 million, respectively, as per IC_3, 2020 and the annual cost of online scams had been $10 billion as per IC_3 2020. Further, 50% of scams involved phishing (APWG, 2020). Also, as per Symante, 2020, 25% of internet users experience online scams.

The comparative status of some selected countries/regions belonging to Developed, Developing and Least Developed Countries in respect to illustrative malpractices, frauds, scams etc is enumerated hereunder.

Developed Countries

The amount involved in corruption had been $1.4 trillion as per the report of OECD, 2020; cybercrimes totalled at dollar 200 billion as per Cyber Security Ventures 2020; and money laundering equalled at $800 billion as per UNDC, 2020. Sum of illustrative cases of malpractices relate to US, UK and Canada. In US, 25 percent of medical malpractice claims result in actual payouts, as per National Practitioner Data Bank, 2020. Likewise, as per NHS Resolution, 2020, 12% of NHS claims relate to malpractice in UK. In Canada 20% of medical practice claims result in payouts as disclosed by Canadian Medical Protective Association, 2020.

As per ACFE, 2020 the total volume of frauds had been equal to $2.5 Trillion. Of these, US accounted for $300 billion frauds on account of annual cost of health care (NHS, 2020); UK for £140 billion as annual cost of fraud (National Crime Agency 2020), and Australia for $2.5 billion as annual cost of financial frauds (Australian Institute of Criminology, 2020).

Scams aggregated to $5 billion in developed countries as a whole as per IC_3 2020. In US, UK and Canada the annual cost of online scams had been $ 3.5 billion (FTC, 2020), £2 billion (Action Fraud, 2020) and CAD $1.5 billion (Canadian Anti Fraud Centre, 2020), respectively.

Developing Countries

Corruption amounted to $ 1.1 Trillion (Transparency International, 2020), cybercrimes to $150 billion (Cyber Security Ventures, 2020) and Money Laundering $500 billion (UNODC, 2020), respectively.

Malpractices were reported by 31% of patients experiencing medical negligence in India (National Human Rights Commission, 2019); 25% of medical claims resulted in actual payouts in Brazil (Brazilian Ministry of Health, 2020); and, 20% of medical claims, resulted in actual payouts in South Africa (South African Medical Research Council, 2020).

Frauds aggregated at $1.8 Trillion as per the Report of ACFE, 2020, in developing countries. In these the share of India, Brazil and South Africa has been equal to 1.4 Trillion Rupees (RBI, 2020), R $ 100 billion (Brazilian Federal Court of Accounts 2020) and ZAR 150 billion (South African National Prosecuting Authority, 2020), respectively

The scams in developing countries totalled at $ 3 billion as per IC_3, 2020. Of these online scams worth Rs. 10,000 crores were organized in India (Indian Cyber Crime Coordination Centre, 2020) and R $ 1 billion in Brazil (Brazilian Federal Police, 2020), and ZAR 1 billion in South Africa (South African Cyber Security Hub, 2020).

Least Developed Countries[10]

The corruption amounted to $ 400 billion (UNODC, 2020) in LDCs taken together. Region-wise 50% of countries in Sub-Saharan Africa and 40% of countries in South Asia experienced significant corruption.

Cyber Crimes and Money Laundering aggregated to $50 billion (Cyber Security Ventures, 2020) and $200 billion (UNODC, 2020), respectively. The status of malpractices had been as thus: 40% of health care facilities lack basic amenities (WHO, 2019) in the region of Sub-Saharan Africa and 30% of patients reported that they are experiencing medical negligence (WHO, 2019). Total frauds amounted to $500 million (ACFE, 2020) and the total of scams has been $1 billion as per IC_3, 2020.

7. COMPETITION AND JEALOUSY

COMPETITION

Competition is a situation where individuals or groups strive for common goals, resources or recognition. From individuals or groups, it may spread among different units of an industry and may also spread among akin units found operating at national, regional or even at global level. Depending upon the nature of product/ service, this competition may relate to variety of factors such as market/s, human resources, financial/investment, infrastructure, R&D efforts, institutions, health and education, labour market, technological readiness, macro-economic environment etc.

Covering different parameters, several global, national and regional level institutions have computed Competition Index Ranking.[11] Major Global Competition Index Rankings are depicted as under:

1. Singapore- 84.6
2. Hongkong SAR - 8.2
3. Netherland - 82.4
4. Switzerland - 82.2
5. United States - 81.7
6. Canada - 81.4
7. Germany - 81.3
8. Australia - 81.2
9. Japan - 80.6
10. United Kingdom - 80.5

The Region-wise and Country Category Wise status of Competition Index has been as described below.

Region-wise Competition Index

1. North America - 74.4
2. Europe - 73.4
3. Asia-Pacific - 72.6
4. Latin America - 68.2
5. Middle East & North Africa - 66.4
6. Sub-Saharan Africa - 64.9

Competition Index by Country Type

1. Developed Economies - 78.2
2. Developing Economies - 69.2
3. Least Developed Countries - 61.4

'Competition' may be healthy as well as unhealthy. If healthy, it will be incremental to growth or else it may harm economic growth of the concerned country/ or even at global level. To illustrate, it encouraged innovations and building resilience (World Economic Forum 2020 and Global Entrepreneurship Monitor 2020). 85% of companies reported that their innovations have been due to competition (WEF, 2020); 75% of entrepreneurs reported that they have been helped by competition in building resilience (Global Entrepreneurship Monitor, 2020). The OECD reported that 20% of GDP growth has taken place due to competition.

Unhealthy competition, likewise, created stress in the 60% employees of US (American Psychological Association, 2020), 40% of companies report witnessing unethical behaviour due to competition (Ethisphere Institute, 2020) and as per IMF (2020) 30% of countries report increased income inequality due to competition.

Country-type Picture

Developed and Emerging countries

In US, high competition (8.5/10) encouraged innovation and entrepreneurship; the medium competition (6.5/10) balanced innovation and social welfare in Germany, and low competition (4.5/10) prioritized social harmony over competition in Japan. Again, in China, high competition (8/10) facilitated economic growth and innovation, medium competition (6/10) balanced growth and social welfare in India and low competition (4/10) struggled with corruption and inequality in Brazil.

On industry specific front the high competition (9/10) resulted in rapid innovations and disruption in the sphere of technology, the medium competition balanced innovation and regulation in the area of finance and low competition prioritized patient care in health care sector. The illustrative statistics for consequences of unhealthy competition is as thus: 50 per cent of employee experienced burnout due to competition (Gallup, 2020); 30% of companies reported corruption due to competition (Transparency International, 2020) and 25% of countries reported increase in income inequalities due to competition (IMF, 2020). These unencouraging results could be taken care of *via* encouraging collaborations, fostering ethical cultures and promoting social welfare activities.

JEALOUSY

Jealousy is a complex emotion characterized by feelings of insecurity, resentment and anxiety due to perceived threats to relationships, status or possessions. Though we have tried to deal with it as part of human values, yet it operates globally, transcending cultural and geographical boundaries. According to a study published in the Journal of Personality and Social Psychology, 75% of people experience jealousy at point in their lives (2018). A survey conducted by You Gov. found that 44% of Americans, 42% Britons and 38% of Australians reported feeling jealous in 2020.

Variety of factors contribute towards enhancement of this emotional state of affair. Important among these are social and psychological factors. Irvin in a study by the University of Californica found that use of social media increases jealousy by 25% (2019). Similarly, the Pew Research Centre (2020) found that 60% of people feeling jealous when they see others', relationships on social media. Insecure attachment styles are responsible for 30% of jealousy cases (Journal of Personality and Social Psychology, 2018). Further, low self-esteem and narcissistic tendencies increase jealousy by 20% (Psychological Science, 2019).

While complete data is not available in respect to the consequences caused by jealousy, still we may peruse same relevant details in the context. The global cost of jealousy related crimes, such as domestic violence and stalking is estimated to be $1.4 Trillion per annum (WHO:2019). Jealousy related workplace conflicts result in an estimated decrease of 10% in productivity and 5% increase in employees turnover (Society for Human Resource Management, 2019).

Some country specific Data can also be pursused. 22% of homicide case in USA are jealousy related (FBI, 2020). One in 5 relationships experience jealousy related abuse in UK (UK office for National Statistics 2020). In India 40% of married women experience jealousy related violence (National Family Health Survey, 2019-20). And, in China 25% of couples report experiencing jealousy related conflicts (Chinese National Bureau of Statistics, 2020).

In order to mitigate the situation both the UNO and WHO has taken some initiatives by emphasising on gender equality, violence reduction and mental health and substance abuse. Other strategies which can be integrated in human values could be Communication and Trust Building, emotional intelligence and self-awareness and couples therapy.

As AI is gradually assuming 'vital role' in leading technological developments which needs special attention. Hence, a full-fledged discussion on it has been attempted in Chapter: 4.

******

ENDNOTES

1. Source: Worldometer, page 1, November 17, 2024, World Population Clock, United Nations Organization.
2. In Asia, China and India are the 2 most populous countries, with 1.4 billion people each and thus accounting for 18% of the world's total population.
3. Africa is the fasted growing continent with more than half of global population growth between now and 2050.
4. GNI and GDI also often used interchangeably but for being precise it will be noted that GNI includes income from foreign investments while GDI does not include these. The data included herein pertain to the year 2022 and the sources have been the World Bank 2022, IMF and UNDP (United Nations Development Programmes).
5. The data for both the "Lower-Middle-Income" group countries ($1026 - $4035) and "Upper-Middle-Income" group countries ($4036-$12,475) have been clubbed under the heading developing countries.
6. The prime sources of statistics have been UNESCO Institute for Statistics, World Bank, OECD, PISA & UNDP.
7. STEM stands for Science, Technology, Engineering and Mathematics And STEM education encompasses careers in: **Science:** Biology, Chemistry, Physics and Environmental Science; **Technology:** Computer Science, Information Technology, Data Analysis; **Engineering:** Mechanical, Electrical, Civil Engineering, Aero-space and Biomedical; and **Mathematics:** Pure Maths, Applied Mathematics, Statistics and Acturial Science.
8. For detailed description of how Technology Trends are deriving innovation, please read ERIC EKUDDEN, Senior Vice President at Group CTO: https://www.ericsson.com/en/reports-and-papers/ericsson-technology-review/articles/technology-trends-2017.
9. Phishing Scam, Ponzi Schemes or Online Romance Scams are some popular examples.
10. The supportive data/information has been gathered from different reports of World Health Organization (WHO), Association of Certified Fraud Examiners (ACFE), International Chamber of Commerce (ICC), Transparency International, United Nations Office on Drugs and Crime (UNODC), Cyber Security Ventures and Internet Crime Complaint Centre (IC_3).

11. Major Institutions include: International Institute for Management (IMD Business School) published its World Competitive Year Book, 2024, World Bank, Niti Aayog, OECD (Organization for Economic Cooperation and Development), World Economic Forum, IMF and National Statistical Services.

CHAPTER - 3

CONTEMPORANEOUS OPTIMISM: EMERGENCE OF ARTIFICIAL INTELLIGENCE (AI)

The data/ statistics/ information contained in the foregoing chapters lead us to two important findings. One, it is only about 60% of the total countries of the world which are making meaningful contribution towards their growth. And for this, these countries, their leaders and systems feel affectation. Those which could not attempt to blame nature, climate, environment, geo-political status, inadequate natural resources, illiteracy and other limitations as the prime reasons. Two, this contribution, a major portion of which is from the developed and upper-middle-income group of developing countries, has however not been completely free from non-ethical and non-human-values oriented. It is stitched with numerous business malpractices, financial frauds, corruption, cybercrimes, scams and money laundering. Not only these, the technological advancements have been accompanied with the development of Artificial Intelligence – the tool which is witnessing a much faster development and never thought of applications which are likely to threaten humans and the world as a whole. Hence this chapter is concentrated only on the developments in the field of AI, and the shape it is likely to assume in future.

ARTIFICIAL INTELLIGENCE (AI): ITS EMERGENCE AND THE PICTURE AS OF 2024[1]

AI first emerged in early 1950 when symbolic logic and rule-based systems were used to generate logical conclusions. Another important step included **artificial neural network,** capable of performing pattern recognition by learning from data through interactive optimisation. The advancements in these computational-intense algorithms, have progressed in performance and cost, through the evolution of computing power, data availability and connectivity. The advances that have taken place in the broad field of AI till the close of 2023 can be summarized as under:

A decade ago, the best AI systems in the world were unable to clarify objects in images at human level. AI struggled with language comprehension and could not solve mathematics problems. Today AI systems routinely exceed human performance on standard benchmarks, including some in image clarification, visual resourcing and English Understanding. Thus, AI now beats humans on some tasks, but not on all. It trails behind on more complex tasks like competition level mathematics, visual common sense, reasoning and planning.

Among countries, the United States have been the leading source of top AI models followed by China, the EU and the UK. In 2023, 61 notable AI models originated from US based institutions, far outpacing the Europeans Union's 21 and China's 15. However, there has been significant progress in respect to growth of AI models during the year 2024[2]. The exact number and the status of the aforesaid countries, however, is yet to be known[3].

In so far as AI research is concerned, it is mostly done at industry level vis-à-vis academia level. In 2023, industry produced 51 important machine-learning models *vis-à-vis* 15 by academia. However, 21 models resulted from industry – academia collaborations. The number of research institutions/ organisations in US, China and EU are 1500, 2000 and 1000, respectively. Top US AI hubs are Silicone Valley, Boston and New York City. In EU the top AI hubs are London, Berlin and Paris. And, in China, Beijing, Shanghai and Shenzhen are top AI hubs.[4]

Contribution of AI in advancing scientific discoveries is also on a continuous upward direction. In past two years there has been significant new launch of science related AI applications. For example, AlphaDev which makes algorithmic sorting more efficient, and GNoME which facilitates the process of materials discovery. Even so, Robust and standardized evaluation, for LLM responsibility are seriously lacking. Also, new research undertaken reveals a significant lack of standardisation in responsible AI reporting.

As per AI index estimates, the training costs of state-of-the-art AI models are quite high. Thus, the open AI's GPT4 used an estimated $78 million worth of compute to train, while Google's Gemini Ultra Cost $ 191 million for compute.

The studies carried out for adjudging the impact of AI on labour reveals that is enables workers to complete tasks more quickly, aside improving the quality of their output. Thus, AI makes workers more productive and leads to high quality work. These studies also demonstrated AI's potentials to bridge the skill gap between low and high skilled workers. However, some other studies caution that AI should not be used without proper oversight.

The total investments in AI, both private and public are expected to reach $632 billion by 2028 with a forecasted compound annual growth rate (CAGR) of 29 per cent from 2024 to 2028. This growth is driven by the increasing adoption of AI technologies across different industries including financial services, software and information services and in retail. In respect to geographical distribution of this investment it may be mentioned that United States is expected to be the largest geographic region for AI investment accounting for more than half of all AI spending, followed by Western Europe and China[5].

Although not exactly contextual in view of the title of this work, yet for the sake of those who might be interested in the status of India in respect to AI, a brief note has been added among endnotes of this chapter.[6]

THE FUTURE OF AI

While there is no doubt that there is a remarkable potential in AI to dramatically affect the lives of the people in next decade, but it could be both ways i.e., for good and bad. The survey from IPSOS[7] revealed that the proportion of those who think AI will dramatically affect their lives in next 3 to 5 years has increased to 66 per cent in 2023 over 60 per cent in 2022....52 per cent expressed their nervousness toward AI products and services, making a 13%-point rise from 2022. In America, Pew Data[8] suggests that 52% of Americans report feeling more concerned than excited about AI

It's with this backgrounds that the recent UN **'Summit for the Future'**, held on September 22 and 23, 2024 at its Head Quarters in New York, concluded that one of the focus area would be "Global Digital Compact" in order to facilitate development of "An Open, free, secure and human centered Digital Future Anchored in Human Rights, Enabling the Sustainable Development Goals". Before we move ahead to add an elaboration on this 'Compact', let us reproduce some of the observations included in the Thailand's Newspaper, Bangkok Post of September 20, 2024 concerning "Development of AI". The UN Secretary General established a panel of 40 experts from the field of technology, law and data protection. This panel, in their report submitted in October 2024, made certain observations which are of paramount importance: "The development of AI should not be guided by market forces alone .... calling for the creation of tools for global cooperation". Their report published days before the start of "Summit of the Future" raised the alarm over the lack of global governance of AI as well as the effective exclusion of developing countries from debates about "technology future". Of the UN's 193 members, just seven are part of the seven major initiatives linked to AI, while 118 are entirely absent-mostly the nations of global south. **"There is, today, a global governance deficit with respect to AI, which by its nature is cross-border",** the experts warn in their Report. **"AI must serve humanity equitably and safely"**, Secretary General of UN said just a day before the Summit. **"Left unchecked, the dangers posed by AI could have serious implications for democracy, peace and stability."** Hence, the experts called on UN members **"to put in place mechanisms to grease the wheels of global cooperation on the issue, as well as to prevent unintended proliferation....the development, deployment** and use of such **a technology cannot be left on the whims of markets alone"**,[9] the report says. Hence, a distinct policy brief was adopted by UN. The contents of this brief are summarised hereunder.

GLOBAL DIGITAL COMPACT OF UN: THE DETAILS OF POLICY BRIEF[10]

Purpose: It sets out principles, objectives and actions of the Global Digital Compact with a view to harnessing the benefits of digital technologies for all and putting in place guardrails and governance to prevent their misuse.

Background: Our digital world is one of stark divides: a persistent digital access divide across regions, gender, income, language and age groups; growing data divides that disadvantage developing countries; and an innovation devide resulting in highly unequal wealth generation, dominated by a handful of big platforms and states. Behind these devides, a massive governance gap. New technologies lack basic guardrails, and public administrations are not well equipped to support the rapid digital transformations of society.These developments have not only brought unparallel opportunities but also pose enormous risks, necessitating global multi stakeholder cooperation. It is essentially urgent to close the digital divide to avoid fracture of the global digital community, make the online space open and safe for everyone, and govern new technologies and artificial intelligence (AI) for all of humanity.

ACCELERATING THE SUSTAINABLE DEVELOPMENT GOALS

Digital technologies have proven potential to advances progress across the Sustainable Development Goals. We need to harness data at scale, make them globally accessable and use them to inform actions across all the goals. For example, adopting global environmental data standards will be critical for enabling action to address the triple planetary crisis.

Recommendations

1. **Digital Connectivity & Capacity:** Targets, policies and tracking for affordable, meaningful, universal connectivity, with financing for hard to reach areas, education for digital literacy and skills and a capacity development network, among other things.
2. **Digital Cooperation for the Goals:** Scaled up investment in safe inclusive digital public infrastructure with support for digital transformation, data and innovation across the Goals.
3. **Upholding Human Rights:** Steps to ensure legal commitments are applied online, including by establishing a digital human rights advisory mechanism to provide guidance.
4. **Inclusive, Open, Secure & Shared Internet:** Commitment to safeguard the free and shared nature of the Internet, so as to avoid blanket internet shutdowns, and to refrain from damaging or destroying critical infrastructure, among other things.
5. **Digital Trust and Security:** Address harmful online content through common standards, guidelines, oversight and industry codes of conduct, while respecting freedom of expression.
6. **Data Protection and Empowerment:** Give people the ability to manage their own data, through common definitions and standards, legal protections for personal data and privacy and a declaration on data rights and principles for data governance, among other things.
7. **AI and Emerging Technologies:** Ensure AI and other emerging technologies are safe, under human control and governed fairly and transparently. A high-level advisory body on AI will be urgently convened to offer recommendations by the end of year on governance that will promote the ethical use of AI that is aligned with human value and human rights.

8. **Digital Commons & Implementation:** Sustained multi-stakeholder cooperation through existing digital forums and an annual Digital Cooperation Forum that supports exchange, shared learning and aligned action across them.

Thus, this compact concluded:

"We urgently need to find ways to harness digital technologies for the benefit of all. We need national and international governance arrangements that prevent their misuse. We must shape innovation in ways that reflect universal human values and protect the planet."

*****

ENDNOTES

1. Source, 'Artificial Intelligence Index Report, 2024', Stanford University, USA.
2. Estimated number of AI models developed in the US between January 2024 and October, 2024 varied between 5000-7000 as per conservative estimate and between 10,000-15,000 as per liberal estimate; in China this number varied between 8000-12000 and 15,000-20,000 and in EU between 3000-5000 and 6000-10,000, respectively.
3. Due to the rapidly evolving AI landscape, private and proprietary nature of AI research, and varied definitions of "AI Model".
4. The Sources of information being National Science Foundation, 2024 for US; and Ministry of Science of Technology, 2024 for China; and, European Patent Office, 2024 for EU.
5. Source: Worldwide Spending on Artificial Intelligence Forecast by International Data Corporation (IDC, August 19, 2024).
6. The growth of AI in India is expected to skyrocket, reaching $9.6 billion by 2032, with a compound annual growth rate (CAGR) of 29.1 percent from 2024 to 2032. This rapid expansion is driven by several key factors, including the Country's vast pool of skilled STEM talent, proactive government initiatives, and increasing demand for AI-driven solutions across various industries (Source: India Artificial Intelligence Market Size, Trends-2032). Top Indian Cities for AI Development are Bengaluru: 1500 + AI Models; Delhi NCR: 1000+ AI Models; Hyderabad: 500+ AI Models: and, Mumbai: 400+ AI Models.
7. A global market Research firm.
8. Pew Research Centre is another Data Tank in USA.
9. See, please Bangkok Post, News Paper, Thailand, September 20, 2024.
10. www.un.or/en/common-agenda/policybriefs.

CHAPTER - 4

CAUSES OF WORRY: AI'S MISUSES, WARS AND CONFLICTS AMONG DIFFERENT NATIONS

The development of newer and newer models of AI taking place at accelerated speed.[1] The investment is going up and up. The scope of AI's application is rapidly expanding. The standards of efficiency, quality and productivity are rising with the lapse of reducing time span. New AI enabled job opportunities are being created. Even so, the latest scenario of AI misuse is quite alarming. Experts warn that AI can be sued maliciously by rogue states, criminals and terrorists, disrupting digital, physical and political stability. On the whole, the misuse of AI has led to significant consequences worldwide. Available information concerning this aspect may be seen below.

(i) **Cyber Attacks:** AI can be subjected to launch automated backing attacks, impersonate targets through speech synthesis, and send finely targeted spam e-mails.

(ii) **Surveillance:** AI-powered analytics can be used to aggregate, analyze and act on citizen data, threatening privacy and individual freedom.

(iii) **Autonomous Weapons:** AI can be used to develop autonomous weapons, systems, potentially violating international law and ethical principles. This raises concern about major risks to civilians and the potential for these weapons to fall into wrong hands.

(iv) **Fake News & Propaganda:** AI generated deep fakes can be used to manipulate public opinion and spread misinformation. AI generated images, videos, and audio clips have made it difficult to distinguish between credible and faulty news, posing a huge issue for society. AI algorithms can thus also influence elections and political discourse.

(v) Bias & Discriminations: AI bias goes beyond gender and race, with algorithms amplifying existing prejudices and potentially exacerbating societal issues like housing discrimination.

(vi) Data Privacy: The lack of regulation regarting AI-collected data poses significant concern for data privacy and security.

(vii) Job Losses: By 2030 tasks accounting for up to 30 percent of hours worked in the US economy could be automated. And, as per Goldman Sachs estimates 300 million full time jobs could be lost due to AI automation.

(viii) Financial Crises: Algorithmic trading could lead to market volatility and financial crises, as seen in 2010 Flash Crash and Knight Capital Flash Crash.

The above description of AI's misuse, highlights the urgent need for its regulation and responsible development in order to mitigate its risks and ensure that its benefits are shared equitably.

MAJOR WARS/ CONFLICTS

Despite all efforts, the world is facing several wars and conflicts. The current global conflicts, land scape is complex and multifaceted. However, we may like to make a reference to the ongoing major wars and Notable Conflicts in the Context.[2] These include: Myanmar Civil War; Arab-Israel; Insurgency in Maghrab; Mexican Drug War; Russian Ukraine conflict; The Yemen Civil War; The Syrian Civil War; The Kashmir Conflict; Israeli Palestinians; Rohingya Conflict; The Sudan conflict; the Ethiopia Conflict; the Congo Conflict; Pakistan Conflict; Bangladesh Conflict; Canada Conflict, etc. Region-wise the number of on going conflicts is or thus:

1. **Middle East of North Africa:** Over 45 armed conflicts;
2. **Africa:** More than 35 around conflicts;
3. **Asia:** 21 armed conflicts;
4. **Europe:** 07 armed conflicts; and
5. **Latin America:** 06 armed conflicts.

All put together, wars/conflicts-total up to 150.

*****

ENDNOTES

1. "The Top Artificial intelligence Trends in 2024", IBM: www.ibm.com.
2. The detailed description of these wars/conflicts may be seen in Chapter 10 of this Study.

CHAPTER – 5

GLOBAL AND REGIONAL INSTITUTIONAL FRAMEWORK: MAJOR CONTRIBUTIONS

One more gap needs to be filled in before we shift to our prime aim. We do have an elaborate international and regional setup to resolve the problems of the world's population.The setup as of now is comprised of UNO, IMF, World Bank, WHO, WTO, G20, G7, EU, ASEAN, AU, Organization of American States, SAARC and BRICS International Inter-Governmental Organization. While it may not be feasible to detail out here the working and contribution of each institution/regional block, we do attempt here to mention the same in brief.

UNO (United Nations Organization): The UNO has played significant role since its establishment on October 24, 1945 to promote peace, security and cooperation among its member states. Its major contributions have been as thus:

- Prevented many conflicts and maintained international peace through mediating disputes, negotiating peace agreements and deploying peace keeping missions;
- Promoted decolonization and independence for many nations;
- Established international human rights standards;
- Provided humanitarian aid to millions;
- Supported global health initiatives and eradicated diseases like Smallpox, Covid, etc.;
- Assisted establishment of United Nations Educational, Scientific and Cultural Organization (UNESCO), World Food Organization (WFO), International Labour Organization (ILO), WTO and WHO in order to strengthen its own functioning;

- Established Global Governance institutions: (i) **G20:** A forum for the world's leading economies to discuss global economic issues, and (ii) **G7:** A group of seven major industrialized countries that meet to discuss global economic and security issues;
- Setting targets for SDGs and for poverty reduction, education and healthcare as part of Millennium Development Goals (MDGs);
- Coordinating global responses to climate change for the purpose of climate change mitigation;
- Promoting nuclear non-proliferation and disarmament;
- Providing humanitarian aid and protection to refugees and displaced persons;
- Coordinating global efforts to prevent and respond to terrorism;
- Warning and responding to potential genocides;
- Promoting gender equality and protecting vulnerable groups; and,
- Addressing global environmental challenges.

The UNOs contributions are likely to go up and deeper in all the aforesaid areas as per the latest Summit held in September 2024. Not only it aims to forge a new international consensus on delivering a better present, but it also intends to safeguard the future. Accordingly, the diverse stakeholder[1] gathered in thousands on September 20 and 21, 2024 for determining the **"Future Action Days"**. It was followed by the "Summit of the Future" on September 22-23, 2024. It is in this, the world leaders adopted the landmark **"PACT for the Future"**[2] that includes a 'Global Digital Compact'[3] and a 'Declaration on Future Generations'. This pact consists of 56 actions designed to **"turbocharge"** the SDG, particularly in areas like peace and security, global governance, climate change, and human rights.

Global Digital Compact is the first comprehensive global framework for digital cooperation and AI governance which aims to connect all people, schools and hospitals to the internet and ensure a safe online space. The declaration on future generations is a commitment to provide more meaningful opportunities for young people to participate in decision making processes.

Between September 24 to 27, 2024 the UNO's Higher Level Week came to be organized in the form of High-Level Meetings such as SDG

Moment, General Debate, High Level Meeting on Sea-level Rise and High-Level Meetings on Antimicrobial Resistance. The SDG Moment highlighted the inspiring examples of progress made towards achieving the SDGs, emphasing the role of just and inclusive transitions in accelerating progress. High-level Meeting on Sea-level Rise addressed the urgent threat of rising sea levels and the need for promoting international cooperation and comprehensive solutions. And, the necessity of renewed efforts for combating the growing threat of antimicrobial resistance and ensuring accountability and strengthening health systems came to be highlighted in the High Level Meeting on Antimicrobial Resistance. In between on September 26, 2024, UN observed the International Day for the Total Elimination of Nuclear Weapons with the clear goal of removing the threat of Nuclear War via organizing a high – level plenary meeting of the General Assembly. However, the overall contribution of UNO could only be judged by the following observations of its General Secretary, Anto Guterres:

"We cannot build a future for our grandchildren with a system built for our grandparents."

WHO and WTO

World Health Organization (WHO) show its establishment on April 7, 1948 for promoting global health, preventing diseases and improving quality of life as a specialized agency of the UNO. It is Head Quartered at Geneva, Switzerland and has six regional offices. It has played a leading role in several public health achievements, most notably the eradication of smallpox, the near eradication of polio and the development of an Ebola vaccine. Its current priorities include communicable diseases such as, HIV/AIDS, Ebola, Malaria and Tuberculosis; and, non-communicable disease such as heart disease and cancer; healthy diet, nutrition and food security, occupational health and substance abuse. The agency advocates for universal health care coverage, engagement with the monitoring of public health risks, coordinating responses to health emergencies and promoting health and wellbeing generally. Its total approved budget is $6.83 billion for 2024-25, while it stood at $7.2 billion for 2020-21 and $6.2 billion for 2022-23.

WTO (World Trade Organization) appeared on the world's scene on January 01, 1995 for encouraging free trade, reducing tariffs and improving trade rules. Accordingly, it impacted world's international trade in following ways.

- It established a rule-based trading system to promote predictability, stability and fairness.
- WTO's tariff reduction agreements have led to lower trade barriers and increasing trade volumes.
- It acts as a forum for resolving trade disputes between member countries.
- WTO's agreement has liberalized trade in goods and services and thus expanding market access for businesses.
- WTO's Agreement on Trade Related Aspects of Intellectual Property Rights (TRIPs) protects Intellectual Property Rights globally.
- It has promoted standardisation and harmonization of trade regulations thus simplifying international trade.
- It provides technical assistance to developing countries for enhancing their capacity to participate in international trade.
- WTO's Trade Facilitation Agreements (TFA) aims to simplifying and streamline customs procedures.

IMF AND WORLD BANK

IMF (International Monetary Fund) and World Bank came to be established in July 22, 1944 in terns of Bretton Woods Agreement. While the IMF's primary objective has been to promote monetary cooperation and exchange rate stability, the World Bank is expected to reduce poverty and promote sustainable development. With the total lending of $1.3 Trillion (since 1944) and an average annual lending ranging between $50-60 billion, the IMF has been thus playing a crucial role in maintaining global financial stability through monitoring economic policies and financial systems and providing financial assistance to countries facing economic difficulties. The IMF, it may be noted, only acts as a Global Financial Safety Net *via* providing emergency funding for short-term.

The identical data in respect to World Bank is as thus. It's total lending aggregated to $2.5 Trillion since 1944 with an average annual lending ranging between $60-$70 Billion for poverty reduction with efforts on the development of infrastructure and human development. The Bank's financial assistance has also supported entrepreneurship and job creation in private sector, aside providing safety nets for vulnerable population.

REGIONAL GROUPS: EU, ASEAN, AU, SAARC, OAS & BRICS

It was on May 25, 1952 that a European Coal and Steel Community Group came to be established, which was converted into EU (European Union) on November 1, 1993 with as many as 27 member countries. Likewise, the Association of Southeast Asian Countries (ASEAN) came into existence on August 8, 1967 with 10 members. First as an Organization of African Unity (OAU) in 1963, which was reorganized as African Union (AU) with as many as 55 members on May 26, 2001. The Organization of American States (OAS) appeared on global map on April 30, 1948 with 35 members. The South Asian Association for Regional Cooperation (SAARC) came to be established on December 8, 1985 with 8 members. On 16 June 2009 with 4 members and with 5th member in 2010, the BRICS (Brazil, Russia, India, China and South Africa) came into existence to promote economic cooperation, global governance reforms, and regional development. In 2023, 6 other members were also added but their membership was announced on January 1, 2024; these members being: Argentina, Egypt, Ethiopia, Iran, Saudi Arabia and UAE (United Arab Emirates). Additionally, 13 more countries were added as partner countries in October 2024. Now this group is known as BRICS international inter-governmental organization. As of January 2025 the BRICS accounted for 46 per cent of world's population of 25 per cent of the World's landmass.

G-20 (Group of Twenty) is now another group of 20 countries, which came into existence in 1999 (September 25, 1999) as a meeting of Finance Ministers and Central Bank Governors which took place in Berlin, Germany for promoting economic stability and cooperation. And in 2008, G-20 was elevated to a Leader's Summit for responding to the global financial crisis. It was on November 15, 2008 that its First Summit was held at Washington DC, USA.

Some other notable regional groups that exist are: **GULF COOPERATION COUNCIL (GCC)** (1981), Economic Community of West African States (ECOWAS) (1975), South African Development Community (SADC) (1980), Eurasian Economic Union (EEU) (2015) and Union of South American Nations (UNASUR) (2008) – this group was however suspended in 2019 due to internal conflicts but was replaced on March 22, 2020 by the Forum for the Progress and Integration of South America (PROSUR).

These Regional and Sub-Regional Groups/ Organizations/ Summits too have made their contributions in promoting economic growth and integration, enhancing regional stability and security, protecting human rights and democracy, addressing global challenges like climatic change and pandemics and in fostering cultural exchange and people-to-people ties. These apart, they have also impacted the different dimensions of global governance in their respective regions and at times between two or more regional groups. Just to illustrate, EU shaped global economic governance, climate change policies and human rights; ASEAN influenced east-asian economic integration, regional security of ASEAN-EU cooperation; AU promoted African Unity, economic integration and global representation; SAARC forstered South Asian Cooperation, Economic Integration and Regional Security; and BRICS emerged as an important global economic bloc influencing international governance.

*****

ENDNOTES

1. This included representatives from member states, civil society, the private sector, academia, local and regional authorities, and youth.
2. The complete pact may be read in Annexture 5 which follows in successive pages of this chapter.
3. Please see, the preceding Chapter 3 for details of Global Digital Impact.

Annexure: 5

UN (UNITED NATIONS) SUMMIT OF FUTURE : AN OVERVIEW OF POLICY BRIEFS

Policy Brief 1: Future Generations

With the specific purpose to fulfil the long-standing commitment to meeting the demands of the present in a way that safeguards the interest of future generations by ensuring that we take decisions with the long-term in mind.

Choices we make today will have consequences for 10 billion people yet to born this century, most in low and middle-income countries, whom we have a duty to protect from foreseeable harms. Hence a special envoy will be appointed in UN to advocate for future generations, the impact of our decisions/actions will be evaluated with better foresight, data and science, members will make a declaration for the future and intergovernmental forum on future generations will provide a locus for debate and collaborations.

Policy Brief 2: Emergency Platform

Member States may provide the Secretary General and the UN System with standing authority to convene and operationalize an Emergency Platform in the event of complex global shocks of significant scale, severity and reach. The Emergency Platform would not, however, displace or duplicate existing mechanisms, but would forces on high-level convening and advocacy, for a finite period, bringing together actors with an ability to contribute meaningfully to the global response.

Policy Brief 3: Meaningful Youth Engagement

Young people are the key to a sustainable break through and have the most to lose if breakdown persists. Hence, more meaningful participation is needed in order to make decision making more effective, innovative and long-term engendering greater trust in public institutions and leading to better outcomes for all. Hence, member states could ensure that meaningful participation of youth is the norm in all United Nations intergovernmental processes and could also support the establishment of a StandingUnited Nations Youth Townhall to provide a dedicated Forum for young people to better prepare for participation in decision-making at the United Nations and to boost the diversity of youth voices informing the work of the United Nations.

Policy Brief 4: Beyond Gross Domestic Product

The brief sets out the process to develop metrics that measure progress and allocate resources on the basis of a fuller picture of what is needed to sustain life of human wellbeing, rather than focusing only on gross domestic product (GDP). Accordingly, three potential actions are called for: a framework to "value what counts"; a value dashboard of key indicators; and, statistical capacity building, and data.

Policy Brief 5: Global Digital Compact

This brief sets our principles, objectives and actions of a Global Digital Compact with a view to harnessing the benefits of digital technologies for all and putting in place guardrails and governance to prevent their misuse. For the purpose this brief contains eight major recommendations, namely;

(i) Digital Connectivity and Capacity;

(ii) Digital Cooperation for the Goals;

(iii) Upholding, Human Rights;

(iv) Inclusive, Open, Secure and Shared Internet;

(v) Digital Trust and Security;

(vi) Data Protection and Empowerment;

(vii) AI and Emerging Technologies: ensuring that these are safe under human control and are governed fairly and transparently; the governance will promote the ethical use of AI that is aligned with human values and rights; and,

(viii) Digital Commons and Implementation.

Policy Brief 6: International Financial Architecture

A fairer, more effective financial system that supports SDG and Climate Action is the need of the day. For the purpose, we have to rebuild trust and prevent further fragmentation of international financial and economic relations. And for this, we need ambitious reforms starting with more inclusive, representative and ultimately more effective global economic governance. Accordingly, actions in six areas are required: Global Economic Governance; Debt Relief and Sovereign Borrowings; International Public Finance; Global Financial Safety Net; Financial System Rules; and, Global Tax Architecture.

Policy Brief 7: Outer Space

With the objective of maximizing benefits and minimizing risks of outer space activities, governance proposal is be worked out so that we can equitably benefit from increase in access to and operations in outer space for achieving the SDGs, while addressing potential risks.

Policy Brief 8: Information Integrity on Digital Platforms

This Brief outlines how threats to information integrity have an impact on global, national and local issues and lays out potential principles for a code of conduct to help guide Member States, the digital platforms and other stakeholders to make the digital space more inclusive and safe for all. It is guiding action to strengthen information integrity on digital platforms. For the purpose, a dedicated capacity will be established in the United Nations Secretariat to scale up the response to online misinformation, disinformation and hate speech, developed tailored communication strategies to anticipate and rapidly address threats before they spiral into online and offline harm and support capacity building of United States Staff and Member States.

Policy Brief 9: A New Agenda for Peace

Collective action is needed to promote peace and prevent conflicts in traditional and potential new domains. Full achievement of the 2030 Agenda for SD is critical. Only 12 percent of the goals are on track. People must be at the centre of our efforts to attain development, overcome poverty and reduce the risks of conflict and violence arising from inequality, marginalization and exclusion. For the purpose 12 Actions-oriented Strategy have been recommended:

Action-1: Eliminate nuclear weapons while strengthening norms and mechanisms against their spread and use.

Aciton-2: Boosting preventive diplomacy to improve geopolitical and geoeconomic relations and guard against incidents in potential new domains, with greater use of United Nation's Offices.

Action-3: Shifting the prevention and sustaining peace paradigm by calling on all States to develop national prevention strategies and by investing in national prevention capacities and infrastructures for peace.

Action-4: Accelerating implementation of the goals to address underlying drivers of violence and insecurity through proven development pathways, new and emerging ways to protect livelihoods and provide social protection, and alignment of international funding mechanisms.

Action-5: Transforming gendered power dynamics in peace and security through concrete measures to secure women's full, equal and meaningful participation in decision-making, eradication of all forms of gender-based violence and sustained, predictable and flexible financing for gender equality.

Action-6: Addressing links between climate, peace and security by ensuring that climate action and peace building reinforce each other. Peace Building Fund be created for financing climate action, resilience and peace building actions.

Action-7: For reducing the human cost of weapons, we need to strengthen protection of civilians in populated areas, achieve universality of treaties banning inhumane and indiscriminate weapons, reduce military expenditures, renew efforts to limit conventional arms, increase investment in prevention and social infrastructures and services, stop the use of improvised explosive devices by terrorists and other non-state armed groups and curb the proliferation of small arms and light weapons and ammunition.

Action-8: Deploying peace operations based on and in support of clearly identified political processes and making peace building more nimble and adaptable.

Action-9: To take up the 'peace enforcement', authorization of the multinational force or action by regional and sub-regional organizations will be needed. Support from United Nations Global Counter Terrorism Coordination Compact may be taken.

Action-10: Support to African Union and sub-regional peace support operations could be ensured by systemically resourcing these *via* United Nations – it is empowered to initiate suitable measures under chapters VII and VIII of its Charter.

Action-11: Promoting novel approaches for preventing the weaponization in emerging domains and encouraging responsible innovations is also the requirement of day.

Cyber Space: Two actions are needed. One declaring the requirements of essential infrastructure for public services and functioning of the society, and two, establishing an independent multilateral accountability mechanism for malicious use of cyberspace by States.

Outer Space: Establishing international norms, rules and principles for addressing threats to space systems and launching negotiations on a treaty to ensure peace, security and the prevention of an arms race in outer space.

Lethal Autonomous Weapons Systems: Concluding of a legal instrument by 2026 is a priority action in order to prohibit lethal autonomous weapons systems which are not in compliance with international humanitarian law. Regulation of all other types of autonomous weapons systems is needed on this pattern.

Artificial Intelligence (AI): We need to develop national strategies on responsible design, development and use of AI and norms, rules and principles on military applications of AI through a multilateral process and agree on a global framework regulating and strengthening oversight mechanisms for the use of data driven technology, including AI, for counter terrorism purposes.

Biological Risks: Reinforcing capacities to identify, anticipate, coordinate and preparing for emerging and evolving biological risks and developing measures to address risks in applying biotechnology and human enhancement technologies in the military domain, including the implications of advances in neurobiology and related converging technologies.

Action-12: Creation of Stronger Collective Security Machinery is needed for making urgent progress on Security Council reform, democratize its procedures and make sanctions, measures more targeted and regularly adjusted, revitalise the General Assembly's role in peace and security, including disarmament and enhance the role of Peace Building Commission.

Policy Brief 10: Transforming Education

This brief put forward a vision and set of guiding actions for countries and the international community to "transform education" for transforming the world *via* creating Learning Societies: **"By Overhauling how we learn, what we learn,**

when we learn, and where we learn and by equipping societies with new skills, capacities and mindsets for a sustainable and just future, we can create the driving force we need to breakthrough a better future for all."

Background: Against a global background of unprecedent wealth and severe inequalities, progress towards securing access to education/quality education for all has faltered. As per estimate made by United Nations over 72 million children of primary education age are not in school, and 759 million adults are illiterate. Further, while the global literacy rate for people aged 15 and above is 99.2% in developed nations, it is only 70.2% in South and West Asia, and only 64% in Sub-Saharan Africa.

In addition, there is insufficient and inequitable investment in education. What is more, as our world grapples with exponential technological change, existential climate challenges and growing polarization, transformated education systems are needed now more than ever for our collective future.

Hence, it is emphasized in this Brief that if we are to achieve Goals by 2030, pivot our world from breakdown to breakthrough and shape the future beyond 2030 towards greater equality, sustainability and peace then education must be fundamentally change. See, please, Annexure 9.1 appeared at the end of Chapter 9; it contains the ultimate suggestions of the author on the broad subject of transformation of education. The transformation of education is critical to guaranteeing the right to quality education and lifelong learning for all. It is a major requirement for building learning societies, countries and international community overall with the skills, knowledge and mindsets needed to break through to a better future for all.

Two-fold actions are needed to do this all: one, **New shared vision**; and two, **Global Public Good**. New shared vision calls for building a comprehensive and integrated system of education and lifelong learning in a world of uncertainty, ensuring equality and inclusion in and through education, making curricula and pedagogies relevant for today and tomorrow, repositioning the role of teachers as creative guides and facilitators and increasing public investment in education and investing more and more equitably and more efficiently in education.

In Global Public Good, we recognise education and lifelong learning as a global public good and therefore supporting its financial cause so that the expenditure on education reaches to the target of 20 per cent of GNI in developing countries.

POLICY BRIEF 11 - UN 2.03

UN 2.0 is concerned with forward-thinking culture and cutting-edge skills for better impact on the members of United Nations. It emphasizes on Forward Thinking Culture, cutting-edge skills for the twenty-first century, shifting capacities, foster internal change and joint diversion.

CHAPTER – 6

MILLENNIUM DEVELOPMENT GOALS [MDGs] AND SUSTAINABLE DEVELOPMENT GOALS [SDGs] OF UNITED NATIONS: AN EVALUATION

It was first in the year 2000 that the United Nations set 8 Millennium Development Goals (MDGs) for improving the lives of billions of people worldwide which were to be achieved by the target date of 2015. These Goals were: (i) Eradication of Extreme Poverty and Hunger; (ii) Achieving Universal Primary Education; (iii) Promoting Gender Equality and Empowering Women; (iv) Reducing Child Mortality; (v) Improving Maternal Health; (vi) Combating HIV/AIDs, Malaria, and other Diseases; (vii) Ensuring Environmental Sustainability; and, (viii) Developing Global Partnership for Development. These Goals were achieved in varying degrees. And, the UNO transitioned from MDGs to 17 Sustainable Development Goals in 2015 as an Universal Call to end poverty, protect the planet, and ensure peace and prosperity for all. The 17 SDGs are:

(1) No poverty
(2) Zero hunger
(3) Good Health and well being
(4) Quality education
(5) Gender equality
(6) Clean water and sanitation
(7) Affordable and clean energy
(8) Decent work and economic growth
(9) Industry, Innovation and infrastructure
(10) Reduced inequalities
(11) Sustainable cities and communities

(12) Responsible consumption and production

(13) Climate action

(14) Life below water

(15) Life on land

(16) Peace, justice and strong institutions

(17) Partnerships for the goals

These goals are interconnected and aim to create a better future for all by 2030. While the **Year 2025** is running, but no satisfactory progress has been attained at almost all the fronts. Just to illustrate, as of 2022, an estimated 8.4 per cent of world's population or around 670 million people, are still living in extreme poverty.[1] Likewise, the current status of zero hunger is alarming, with the global issue of hunger and food insecurity showing an increase since 2015. As of 2022, approximately 735 million people, or 9.2% of the world's population, suffer from chronic hunger, which is a staggering rise compared to 2019.

In case of third SDG (Good Health and well being), while progress has been made in some areas like maternal and child health, communicable diseases, but the number of people suffering from non-communicable diseases, such as cardiovascular disease, cancer, and diabetes remains high. Not only this, significant gaps remain in achieving universal health coverage. In 2021, about 4.5 billion people lacked access to essential health services.

What to talk about Global Education, even the quality education is a pressing concern as yet. Despite efforts to improve education, progress has been slower than required and the COVID-19 pandemic has exacerbated the key challenges found in this field such as (a) lack of access; (b) poor quality of education, gender disparities, digital divides, etc. Also the gender equality is found almost on an identical status. Despite efforts to achieve equality, the world is not on track to meet this goal by 2030. In fact, at the current rate of progress, it will take an estimated 131 years to achieve gender equality worldwide. In respect to availability of clean water and sanitation, as of 2022, 2.2 billion people lacked access to safely managed drinking water, while 3.5 billion lacked safely managed sanitation services. To address this situation the UN has launched SDG 6 Global Acceleration Framework, but it's doubtful whether this too shall achieve universal access to safe and affordable drinking water to all by 2030.

The picture for Affordable and Clean energy is as thus. The world is making progress in these directions, but there is still a long way to go. 675 million people worldwide still lack access to electricity, with 80 per cent of them living in rural areas. Renewable energy sources are becoming increasingly important with 30 per cent of global electricity mix now coming from renewables. Significant disparities in access to electricity continue to exist and huge investments of infrastructure in still needed.

Shifting to diversified goals concerning Economic Growth, the situation is still worse. Multiple crises are threatening the global economy and the pace of progress has slowed down. The global growth rate of real GDP per capita was 2 per cent in 2018, but it's forecasted to slow down due to multiple challenging economic conditions. The global unemployment rate declined to 5.4 per cent in 2022, but the youth unemployment rate remains high, with 22 per cent of young people not in employment, education or training in 2019. Women and youth are disproportionately affected and, of informal employment is on the rise. Consequently, achieving decent work and economic growth are merely dreams and achievable subject to taking care of large number of challenges like job creation, improving resource efficiency in consumption and production, achieving full and productive employment and decent work for all and reducing the proportion of youth not in employment, education or training. The UN has set 12 targets to achieve decent work and economic growth by 2030, but it's quite doubtful that it will be able to achieve the same.

The SD goal concerning Industry, Innovation and Infrastructure too appear to be a mixed bag. As of 2022, 95 per cent of the world's population has access to a mobile broad based network, but some areas remain unserved. The global manufacturing sector has faced stagnation due to geopolitical instability, inflation, logistical challenges, and a broader global economic slowdown. In respect to industrialisation the manufacturing sector rebounded strongly in 2021 post-COVID, but growth has plateaued at around 2.7 per cent since 2022. Global manufacturing value added per capita rose by 16 per cent from 2015 to 2023, reaching $1,922 per capita. However, regional gaps are stark, with Europe and Northern America hitting a record $4,986 per capita, contrasting with stagnant levels of $ 163 in Sub-Saharan Africa.

Innovation: Research and development expenditure as a proportion of GDP has increased from 1.72 per cent in 2015 to 1.93% in 2021. However, many developing economies have R&D expenditure relative to GDP below 1 per cent.

If we dive into the current status of next 3 SDGs (namely, Reduced Inequalities, Sustainable Cities and Communities, and Responsible Consumption and Production), it is found that while inequalities in some countries have reduced, but significant disparities persist; not only this, COVID-19 pandemic has exacerbated existing inequalities, particularly affecting vulnerable populations such as women, children, and marginalized communities. Cities are growing rapidly, with over half of the global population living in urban areas. However, this growth often outpaces the development of infrastructure, services, and housing, leading to issues like urban sprawl, air pollution, and limited public spaces. Not only this, the world is facing significant environmental degradation due to unsustainable consumption and production patterns. Also, food waste remains a significant issue, with 931 million tons of food wasted annually.

As regard the rest of 5 SDGs (Climate Action, Life Below Water, Life on Land, Peace, Justice and Strong Institutions & Partnerships) the present state of affairs too in quite worrysome. Climate action is crucial, and progress has been made, but there in still much work to be done. The goal is to limit global warming to well below 2°C and pursue efforts to limit it to 1.5°C above pre-industrial levels. Unfortunately, global carbon emissions continue to rise, and window for taking action is rapidly closing.

The ocean covers over 70 per cent of our planet, providing food, energy and regulating the climate. However, marine ecosystems face significant threats from pollution, overfishing, and climate change. Likewise, life on land is facing numerous challenges, including deforestation, desertification, and biodiversity loss. The UN has set targets to combat these issues, including restoring degraded forests and promoting sustainable land use. However, progress has been quite slow and continued efforts are needed to protect and preserve our planet's precious ecosystems.

While the SDG 16 focuses on promoting peaceful and inclusive societies, providing access to justices for all and building effective, accountable, financially strong and inclusive institutions at all levels, and SDG 17 emphasizes on strengthening of global partnerships to support the 16 preceding SDGs, the actual status of both of these is much far from satisfactory. An increased violence is gradually becoming the fact. Just to illustrate the year 2022 witnessed a more than 50 per cent increase in conflict-related civilian deaths, largely due to the war in Ukraine alone. The details of the conflicts, as of to day, may be read in Chapter 10; world over almost 150 armed conflicts are going on as of today spread over almost identical number of countries.

Despite some progress in detecting victims of trafficking, forced labour has increased and sexual exploitation numbers have declined but remain a significant issue. Bribery remains a significant problem, particularly in low-income countries, where an average of 22.3 per cent of businesses reported paying bribes to access public services.

In respect to SDG 17, suffice it would be to say that strengthening global partnerships in variegated areas in the form of global cooperation, and financial support has increased, yet its effectiveness and magnitude could at best be considered just marginal in contrast of need.

On different dimensions, the above picture could at best be considered weak, exiguous and imperfect from the angle of time frame, forward thinking and innovative approach on the one hand and with distinguishing degrees of success on the part of United Nations in resolving the varied issues concerned with sustainable development.

*****

ENDNOTES

1. Defines as surviving on less than $2.15 per person per day.

CHAPTER - 7

CONCISE DECOMPOSITION

In the light of the cognition synchronized in the preceding Chapters, UN is found at the top of existing institutional frame which unconcealed every situation and every aspect of failures in a crystal manner[1]. And, then proceeded to adopt an altogether new kit containing innovative measures for attaining much more than SDGs with peace. However, the long history of its establishment divulges the reverse scenario too in respect to its final achievements. Hence the new set of questions: What is wrong with the UN and other international and regional institutions? Why it is happening again and again? Why the world is, though not vocally said, so afraid of its future? Can it lead us to 'disasters' in couple of decades ahead. Prior to examining these questions let us first have the thumbnail sketch.

The UN has not been able to emerge out as effective **as it was conceived at a global level**, due to its inefficient decision making processes, limited representation and voting power for developing and least developed countries, inadequate funding and resource allocation, ineffective enforcement of resolutions and sanctions, bureaucratic inefficiencies and corruption, lack of accountability and transparency, insufficient attention to global economic governance and limited capacity to address emerging new challenges like cyber security, climate change, AI's governance and its possible misuses.

On the funding front we do have IMF, World Bank, IDA and IFC at international level and EIB (European Investment Bank), IsDB (Islamic Development Bank), ADB (Asian Development Bank), AFDB (African Development Bank), and EBRD (European Bank for Reconstruction and Development) at regional front, **yet we find big funding gaps**. Thus for the period 2020-30, gap exist equivalent to \$1.3 Trillion, \$1.2 Trillion and \$1.5 Trillion for infrastructure, climate change and SDGs, respectively. These gaps apart, the functioning of these institutions also suffers from voting power imbalances, limited representation of small and developing countries and inequitable distribution of benefits and resources. They are additionally handicapped by their fragmentation and overlap, inadequate coordination and cooperation and dependence on donor countries for their funds; in the context it would be relevant to mention that IDA accumulates funds only by way of Charities from developed rich countries.

Regional groups too are not able to assume their grandiose role with which these came to be established. This has primarily been due to inequitable distribution of power and influence, limited regional representation and participation, funding constraints, ineffective conflict resolution mechanisms, bureaucratic inefficiencies and corruption, overlapping memberships and conflicting interests, limited capacity to address emerging regional challenges and limited attention to global challenges.

Just to substantiate the above status we may refer to the situation of conflict in Sudan. Conflict in Sudan has recently displaced more than 14 million people or about 30% of population since it broke one in April 2023, creating the world's largest displacement crisis this year, the International Organization for Migration said on October 29, 2024: **"The internal displacement number has hit 11 million. That's up 2,00,000 just since September"**, the United Nations Agency's Director-General, Amy Pope said. **"Another 3.1 million people have travelled across borders to flee the fighting. In total nearly 30% of Sudan's population has been displaced."**[2]

Similarly, the 19th G-20 Summit held in Rio De Janeiro, Brazil on 18th and 19th November 2024 is said to be ended with **'Blame Game'** due to leaders clash over Russia – Ukraine war.[3] COP29 (29th Conference of the parties of the United Nations Framework Convention on Climate Change – UNFCC) Summit was held in Baku, Azerbaijan between November 11 to 22, 2024. In this Conference nearly 200 countries participated (including 77 Developing Countries belonging to G-77 Group and 39 Countries belonging to Alliance of Small Islands States- AOSIS). While several crucial decisions were taken in this Conference, what is significant here to add that the **Alliance of Small Islands States were ready to leave the UN Climate talks** while negotiating for funds, but finally it agreed that developed countries would provide $300 Billion a year until 2035, but this sum was short of the $500 billion in public finances called for. The deal also agreed in principle that $1.3 Trillion in total is needed from public and private sources for developing nations, but no agreement could be arrived at as to where this money would come from and who would pay it[4]. One of the prominent citizen from Hong Kong, Mr. Prime Sermiento, also observed that, "The Agreement reached at 29th Session of COP29.....has disappointed the developing countries that claimed the $300 billion per year climate finance .... as against proposed $1.3 Trillion in annual assistance"[5]. Likewise, independent High Level Expert Group on Climate Finance has said **"the annual $300 billion per year pledge by 2035 falls short significantly by at least $390 billion a year by 2035 needed to deliver the goals of the Paris Climate Pact."**

Let us also look at the compendium of 16th BRICS Summit held in October 2024. It may be of interest to note about it that "the proposal for rapidly expanding its membership came to be unacceptable to all of its members." But then a solution to this could be found in accepting some of the countries as 'Partner Countries'. Also, it discussed at length for taking initiatives for reducing the global reliance on the US Dollar based on international financial and payment system. And it is the outcome of this discussion that BRICS+Countries have shown an increased preference for monetary gold as an alternative to currency reserves, trading with each other, de-dollarizing their financial flows and maintaining a stable control on foreign exchange reserves. All this, however, also demonstrate the respect which one group of countries has for other countries/ other groups of countries and the US Dollar still remains the **de facto** currency despite BRICS igniting the de-dollarization process.

Let us now shift to the passionate examination of the questions raised in para one of this Chapter. On analyzing the why and wherefore ineffective roles, be it UN, other institutional set up or regional groups, the overriding conclusion lies in identical situations within which they are finally engulfed to operate. In the context, it is possible, or has always been the case, to suggest a couple of measures but the historical perspective concerning the implementation of suggestions given from time to time and the consequential emerging scenarios more than reveals, rather authentically, that the state of affairs have remained unchanged and **"actions taken"** have remained **"actions on paper"** save that there have only been addition (s) to the then prevailing adverse situations which have courageously forwarded with one or the other justification taking side of one or the other cause (s).

Instead of improving, the existing set up is further going to worsen in the light of emerging new challenges as narrated now, namely, climate change and sustainability, cyber security and digital governance, global health and pandemics, economic inequality and instability, migration and refugee crisis, terrorism and violent extremism, nuclear proliferation and disarmament and human rights and humanitarian law. We may recapitulate certain recent developments concerning 'AI-misuses'. Between 2019 and 2021, regulatory initiatives were taken namely, EU's AI Regulation (2021), US's AI Initiative (2020), China's AI Governance Guidelines (2020) and IEEE's Ethics of Autonomous & Intelligent Systems (2019)[6]. Despite these AI misuses threatened the security and surveillance arrangements, aside social media manipulation, generation of fake news, fake videos and audio, tax evasion and market manipulations, financial frauds/scams, etc. And consequently, AI misuses caused monetary losses equivalent to estimated $13.4 Trillion in 2020. During the period 2021 and 2024 too, the monetary losses have been substantial but its aggregate figure is not available. Some recent examples of AI misuses are:

- **Zillow's AI-powered Home Buying Disaster:** Zillow's algorithm led to $304 million inventory write down in 2021.
- **Amazon's AI-enabled recruitment tool:** Amazon's system was scrapped after it was found to be biased against women.
- **Microsoft's Chatbot Debacle:** Microsoft's Chatbot's, TAY, was taken down after it began posting racist and misogynistic tweets.

Can we just make a short halt here! Presume everything goes well for UN, International Institutions and Regional Groups and we are able to make this setup an effective mechanism to attain the sustainable Growth with peace, then we can continue depending upon the United Nations System with Twenty First Century expertise and organizational Culture to deliver stronger results, better support for Member States and faster progress towards the Sustainable Goals.

But for a moment dare say that **the history of ineffectiveness and failures repeats in successive period up to 2030 and thereafter then this era is not likely to last long.** Prior to its burst out it may most likely to witness technological advancements at a fast pace, including the development of newer and newer models of AI (covering the chances of hypothetical development of superintelligence AI models), variable growth rates among different countries of the world, inequitable distribution of wealth, political and economic dominance of certain countries, variety of conflicts among different regional groups, increasing level of malpractices, frauds and scams and the consequent monetary losses affecting different segments of societies/ communities etc. And, the next era, covering say up to beginning of 21st century, most likely to witness World War III[7] which may not be like earlier world wars or World War III accompanied by spread of some specific man-made or other infectious/morbific/ contagious or poisonous endemic which would destroy the most populace of the Earth. It shall be much more that and this "much more" can not be conceived right now. It would be the only contingent happening of the world that we can visibly see due to widespread competitive and jealous feelings among different nations.

To conclude, we may also mention the overriding fact that: we are not the first to warn community about World War III. The UN Secretary General, Antonio Guterres had observed prior to the recent 'Summit for Future' held on September 22 and 23, 2024 in New York that **"we want to hold the Summit in this week in order to avoid moving to World War III."**[8]

*****

ENDNOTES

1. How much UN is transparent could be obvious from the policy brief "UN2.0"? This Policy brief, which was title as 'forward thinking culture and cutting-edge skills for better United Nations System Impact', stated rather frankly, **"the world is not on track to achieve the Sustainable Development Goals. To accelerate progress, everyone needs to re-think, refocus and re-charge. UN 2.0 is a vision of modernized United Nations System, with cutting-edge skills and a forward-thinking culture that enable United Nations Entities to better contribute to the quest for the goals."**
2. China Daily, Newspaper, Global Edition, October 31, 2024, p. 16.
3. Please, read, Bangkok Post, Thailand, November 21, 2024. However, it is also mentioned at G-20 Summit did advance urgent global challenges like economic stagnation, trade disruptions, food security, reform of multilateral institutions and climate governance, besides launching the Global Alliance Against Hunger and Poverty.
4. https://www.bbc.com/news.articles/cpwr/kwz9x90 amp
5. China Daily, News Paper, Global Edition, November 27, 2024, p.10.
6. Some recent AI regulatory initiatives include Sustainable Finance Regulatory Initiatives; Fintech Regulatory Standards, Digital Trade Regulatory Standards, Digital Trade Regulations including e-document and e-signature laws; and World Bank's, Regulatory Governance Initiatives.
7. The Standard Textbooks on Psychology which can be referred to include the following:
   (i) Cialdini, RB, 'Influence Science and Practice', 5th Edition, 2009, Allyn & Bacon.

(ii) Festinger, L. 'A Theory of Cognitive Dissonance', 1957, Stanford University Press.

(iii) Milgram, S. "Behavioural Study of Obedience" Journal of Abnormal & Social Psychology, 67(4), 371-378, 1963.

(iv) Kohlgberg, L. 'The Philosophy of Moral Development', 1988, Harper & Row.

(v) Batson, C.D. 'Altruism in Human', Oxford University Press.

(vi) Khoneman, D., & Tversky, 'Prospect Theory: An Analysis of Decision Making Under Risk 1979, Econometrical 47 (2), 263-292.

(vii) Gazzaniga, M.S., "Human: The Science Behind US Unique', 2008, Harper Collins.

8. Please, see, Bangkok Post, News Paper, Thailand, September 21, 2024, p. 6.

CHAPTER – 8

MIND SHIFT-BEYOND TWENTY FIRST CENTURY

The envisioned tableau of the world would simply be not acceptable to any one, even in dreams. Let us encapsulate a profound transformation with an open, innovative thinking and perspective for a Mind-set Beyond Twenty First Century. Base on our current understanding of historical records, technological advancements, and societal trends, we may argue with confidence that we can treat the period up to Mid-22nd Century (2100-2150) as unhypothetical and upto which educated predictions based on current trends related to growth of cities, renewal energy and expansion of space exploration, etc. be made. As we move further into the 22nd Century and beyond the level of uncertainty and hypothesis increases significantly. The quantum and diversified nature of these uncertainties are forecasted even to cover potential threatening to the human existence, Continent Drifts, fluctuation in earth's climate, changes in the earth's rotation and planet's ecosystems and biodiversity. Putting all at one place, we can briefly say that these uncertainties are likely to have a profound impact on the Earth's habitability and the life forms that may inhabit it. Accordingly, we for this study, confine ourselves to the extended period upto the Mid Twenty Second Century.

Though not extended too a greater timeframe, the Visionary Nations of the world have to realize today that UN and the Global Institutional frame conceived even for 21st century has already reached to the stage of ineffectiveness. The statistics included by us in Chapter-Two till the proceeding Chapter-Seven is a glaring proof of it. These numerical figures apart, the present global scenario is as reported in/by the news papers and other social media is rather fearful and nasty. At Global level, the so considered strong and committed leaders of the world have started talking about ongoing war in Ukraine, bring stability to the Middle East and avert the "Nightmare" of possible Third War.[1] Effort on Re-grouping of the countries is visible, over and above the fully admitted global instability. Violations of UN resolutions by different countries, assuming the realities of the day followed by ethical, human and code of conduct considerations. Corporate leaders, including Elon Musk, have started, expressing their concerns about the potential risks of advanced AI, stating that it could be humanity's **"biggest existential threat"**. **Nick Bostron,** a philosopher and Director of the Future of Humanity Institute, has argued that advanced AI could pose an 'existential risk to humanity. And **Stepten Hawking,** just prior to his passing, warned the world that **the development of AI could spell the end of human race.**

Ergo, the visionary countries of the world like Estonia, United Kingdom, India, Scotland and Wales, may take the lead for immediately constituting a Global Group of catalyst comprising of representatives from UN, other international organizations, civil society movements, and influential group of individuals which can have high level diplomatic meetings on the subject of **supreme global level powerful and effective institution** and can announce its establishment with the name as it may deem fit, e.g. **World Union of Visionary Nations (WUVN)** alongside its membership, objectives and its renewed operational strategy, frame, and set up. The recommendations of this Catalyst Group as visualized and advocated by us are summarized in successive and last Chapter – 9.

ENDNOTE

1. Donald Trump, News 18: https://www.news18.com. World.20.Jan.2025; & One India, https//www.oneindia.com. international.

CHAPTER – 9

WORLD UNION OF VISIONARY NATIONS (WUVN) AND PROGRESSIVE SUSTAINABLE DEVELOPMENT WITH PEACE FOR ALL

The WUVN is being proposed to be established with the enlarged objectives of maintaining **International Peace, Security and Cooperation for Progressively Sustainable Development** in all the member countries. The phrase 'Peace' is to be interpreted to cover (a) absence of conflicts;[1] and, (b) inner calm and harmony. Not only this, this phrase 'Peace' would also embrace **'Peace for All'** which would be **'Inclusive Peace'**, **'Universal harmony'** and **'Social Justice'**.[2]

Thus 'peace' would be an important foundation but 'Peaceful for All', as is being explicitly suggested shall be **more aspirational and inclusive concept** that would seek to create harmonious and just world for everyone. 'Peace for All' shall therefore be distinctly emphasized by WUVN in its strategy and operational tools with the following scope, focus, and implications:

(i) **Scope** – Peace can be individual or localized, while Peaceful for All is a broader and more inclusive concept.

(ii) **Focus** – Peace focusses on the absence of conflict or inner calm, while Peaceful for All emphasizes social justice, equality and universal harmony.

(III) **Implications** – Peace can be achieved through various means, while 'Peaceful for All' requires more comprehensive and inclusive approach addressing systematic issues and promoting change.

PROGRESSIVE SUSTAINABLE DEVELOPMENT

As part of objectives of WUVN, the phrase **'Progressive'** has been added to take care of growth which stands nullified due to 'inflation'. Also it may be added that **Progressive Sustainable Development'** (PSD) is more comprehensive *vis-a-vis* 'Progressive Sustainable Growth.' as the former takes, a more compressive approach addressing broader societal challenges and seeking to create a more just, equitable and sustainable world. PSD thus employs more multidimensional evaluation frameworks, incorporating indicators like human well being, social cohesion, environmental resilience and institutional effectiveness.

OPERATIONAL FRAME

The membership of the WUVN shall be open to all countries of the world and it would be Honorary. There would be a Secretariate headed by Secretary General to look after its day to day functioning. And, this World Union shall meet every year in the shape of its General Assembly. And, it is in its first meeting of the General Assembly that a **Board of Governors** will be constituted of say about 15 to 20 global visionary leaders for a specifically laid down period and other terms of its governance.

Since the actual functioning of this World Union is encapsulated to be guided by a catelogue of experts, it is perceived that it will create and facilitate the establishment and working of expert groups on all of the subjects concerned with it.

EXPERT GROUPS

Accordingly, the WU would create Expert Groups on "Institutional set-up: Global and Regional", "Operational Strategy", "Global Education", "Progressive Sustainable Development Goals", "Global Governance", "AI-Development & Control", "Conflict Resolutions", Climate Change" and "No Wars and Nuclear Weapons – Their Zero-in Process." The recommendations of these "Expert Groups", however, shall not be mandatory to the Board of Governors.

TIME FRAME

The extended time-frame upto Mid-22nd Century can be divided into 3 phases to be continued from 2030, presuming that by that time the Global Group of Visionary Leaders shall be able to complete the formalities required for the establishment of WUVN, its Secretariate, appointment of Secretary-General as also its initial Board of Governors and the constitution of different Expert Groups. Also it will be ensured by the Global Group that the preliminary recommendations of these Expert Groups are available for implementation in the 'Initial Phase-I: 2031-2050" by the World Union of the Visionary Nations. Two other phases would be of 50 years each. Thus Phase II would be from 2051-2100 and it will be known as **'IMPLEMENTATION PHASE'**; and Phase III would be from 2101-2150 and it will be known as **'Mid-term Review and Resurfaced Implementation Phase.'**

RENOVATED INSTITUTIONAL SET UP

With the commencement of Initial Phase: 2031-2050, the first meeting of the Board of Governors will be held and the recommendations of the Expert Group on "Institutional Setup: Global and Regional" shall be discussed and approved finally for immediate implementations. As envisioned by the author, the newly emerged institutional setup would be as thus.

As per renovated set up the IMF would continue to operate on the financial front with its existing objectives, namely, to meet short term emergency monetary needs. But the IBRD, IDA and IFC would be merged in order to create the World Funding Organization (WFO) which would play a much wider role as may be needed for funding the medium and long-term requirements of the different countries of the world aside the funding that may be needed by WUVN for variegated other purposes. The proposed WFO would be a highly empowered institution in matters of mobilizing financial resources. And the WFO would continue to resort to both traditional and innovative methods for raising its funds. **Traditional Methods:** includes issuing of bonds (Global Green and Sustainability Bonds), loan syndications, equity investments, grants from donor countries, interest income from the existing portfolios, and bounties by way of non-refundable funds from rich countries of the world. **Innovative Methods** could be: issuing of Social Impact Bonds (WFO can partner with private sector for funding development projects), Green Finance Instruments (Green Loans Green Sukuk, Climate-resilient Bonds), Impact Investing (collaborate with impact investors for sustainable development), Crowd funding (platforms for citizen engagement and small scale funding), diaspora bonds (tapping the diaspora communities for investment in such bonds), Islamic Finance (Sukuk issuances, Islamic bonds and Shariah – compliant instruments), Public Private Partnerships (PPPs) for infrastructure projects, Blended Finance (combining concessional funding with commercial financing), Philan-thropic Partnerships (collaborating with foundations and philanthropists), and carbon credits (selling carbon credits to support climate friendly projects).

Introducing Digital innovations could constitute still another source for raising fund by WFO. For example, commencement of Blockchain – based platforms for secure and transparent transactions, digital tokens, mobile payment systems and online platforms for crowdfunding and peer-to-peer lending. Some still other methods for raising funds could be *via* resorting to Sustainable Finance instruments like Blue Bonds (Ocean Conservation), Green Blue Bonds (Water Conservation), Climate Resilient Bonds, Progressive Sustainable Development Goals (PSDGs) Bonds, partnering with multilateral development banks (MDBs), collaborating with national development banks, engaging with private sector companies and Team up with NGOs, Civil Society Organizations, increasing subscription-based funding from member countries, introducing a global financial transaction tax and exploring sovereign wealth fund investments.

WHO & WTO

Both of these international organizations shall continue to operate as such excepting that on WUVN assuming its operations then these would operate under its overall supervision and polity directives.

REGIONAL GROUPS

Existing Regional Groups would continue to function as such expecting that these may initiate certain remedial measures for turning their functioning more effective. One, steps for wiping out the over-lapping memberships. Two, reducing the dominance of specific nation(s). Third, making them eligible to borrow funds from WFO on defined terms & conditions. Last but not the least, these groups may seek proactive advice from any of the expert groups(s) but via only WU of Visionary Nations.

OPERATIONAL STRATEGY

With a view to successfully deliver the warranted results, we advocate two basic operational guidelines. **One** to promote **"Capricious Global Education"** in the world. **Second** to implement the Refined **"Progressive Sustainable Development Goals (PSDGs)",** in all countries of the World. While the **"Capricious Global Education"** has been discussed in Part I, the Part II elaborates the Progressive Sustainable Development Goals.

PART – I

CAPRICIOUS GLOBAL EDUCAITON

It would be comprised of necessary inputs of Ethics, Human values, Code of Conduct, STEM, set of skills in all persons, including but not limited to students, working professional, administrators, politicians and individuals from all socio-economic backgrounds, gender, and age groups except of course those who are incapacitated or infants. For students, from nursery to higher education, these inputs shall be in the form of well designed academic courses, at some level theoretical and conceptual but at other higher levels in the shape of applied courses covering real life cases, incidents etc. We are of this firm view that ethics, human valves, code of conduct, put together, must also be included even in competitive examinations conducted for admissions for undergraduate and post-graduate Engineering/Medical and other academic programmers. Not only this, similar course be even included in Competitive Examination held for IAS, IFS, IPS, state level Administrative services. Aside inclusion, these applied courses could also be covered as part of their Training Periods followed for the successful students.

Finally, we are of the considered opinion that the varied inputs of Global Education should continue to be taught all through the active civil services/administrative services, covering services rendered in the business/ corporate would in the shape of One to Three Days Workshops/ Seminars at frequent intervals, say after every 3 to 5 years of gap. However, these inputs would mostly be in the form of case studies/ other academic exercises covering real life happenings/situations concerning different countries of the world. It be added that it's this education which would leads to respect for each other, cooperation and compassionate outlook among people, irrespective of their positions they are occupying, towards their colleagues, companions and neighbouring countries. Even the feelings of competition and jealousy, we are sure, shall be subdued.

The expert group on Capricious Global Education, as suggested above shall continuously work for developing its Academic Courses (both Theory and Applied) for students of different levels of education, Competitive Examinations, Professionals, Politicians, Corporate Executives keeping in view varied socio-economic-political environments found in different countries of the World. Some material on this Capricious Global Education is being included in this Chapter at its end by way of an **Annexure** on: **"CAPRICIOUS GLOBAL EDUCATION."**

PART – II

REFINED PROGRESSIVE SUSTAINABLE DEVELOPMENT GOALS (PSDGs)

Second most vital agenda for the Board of Governors of the World Union of Visionary Nations would be to finalize on priority the refined Progressive Sustainable Development Goals for their implementation in its Initial Phase: 2031-2050 keeping in view the recommendations of the concerned Expert Group. This group has expanded uniformly the time frame upto 2050 for accomplishing the targets set by UNO, but the targets have not been touched by and large in order to provide adequate flexibility to the World Union of Visionary Nations. Also, keeping in view the overriding fact that there exist lot of gap between what has been so far achieved against the laid down targets. However, their nomenclatures have been altered to 'Progressive Sustainable Development Goals', as also couple of new PSDDGs have been added. Further, it may be of interest that it is in next implementation Phase II that the targets may be set up in an upward direction with a view to justify the 'Progressiveness'.

1. **NO POVERTY (PSDG: 1):** In this case, year-after-year the sustainable growth rate of food items, which causes poverty and food insecurity be accelerated, upto the close of 2050. Not alone this, urgent coordinated action and policy-solutions may be necessary in order to address entrenched inequalities, transform food systems and investments in agricultural practices.
2. **ZERO HUNGER (PSDG: 2):** As part of this PSDG, emphasis may be incorporated to end the hunger and malnutrition in South Asia and Sub-Saharan Africa where the populations and demand for food is fastly growing.
3. **GOOD HEALTH & WELL BEING (PSDG:3):** Through PSDG:3, rigorous efforts are needed to achieve the targets already set in respect to (i) Reduction in **'Maternal Mortality';** (ii) **'Preventable Deaths'** of newborns and children under 5; (iii) **Fighting Communicable Diseases;** (iv) reducing mortality from non-communate diseases; (v) **Strengthening** prevention and treatment of mental health disorders; (vi) **Ensuring** Universal access to healthcare services; (vii) **Reducing road traffic** accidents; (viii) **Substantially** reducing the number of deaths and illness from hazardous chemicals and air, water, and soil pollution implementing the **Minamata Convention on Mercury;** (ix) **Supporting** the research and development of vaccines and

medicines; and (xi) **Supporting** the recruitment, development, training, and retention of the health workforce in developing and less developed countries.

The progress has so far been quite meager since 2000 (Maternal mortality decreased by 38%; under-5 mortality decresed by 44 percent; HIV/AIDs new infections decreased by 33 percen, and Tuberculosis and malaria incidences by only 20 percent and 37 percent), the WU for VNs must put in rigorous efforts to take care of present challenges found related to (i) Inequities observed in healthcare access; (ii) Non-Communicable diseases like diabetes, heart disease and cancer; (iii) Mental health; and (iv) the Shortages and inequities found in healthcare workforce distribution.

4. **QUALITY GLOBAL EDUCATION (PSDG:4):** Enough has been elaborated above about this Goal: 4.
5. **GENDER EQUALITY (PSDG: 5):** In respect to this PSDG:5, the WU for VNs needs to pay deeper attentions towards both the number and varieties of key challenges involved, which include: (a) **Discriminatory Laws** -178 countries have legal barriers that prevent women's full economic participation; (b) **Violence Against Women-** One in 3 women globally experienced physical and/ or sexual intimate partner violence; (c) **Limited Access to Education and Health Care Service** to women and girls in quite a good number of countries; (d) **Unpaid care work** – Women spend disproportionately more time on unpaid care work, limiting their economic opportunities.
6. **CLEAN WATER & SANITATION (PSDG: 6):** It aims at ensuring universal and equitable access to safe and affordable drinking water, sanitation, and hygiene (WASH) for all by 2050. While targets have been set for universal access to safe drinking water, sanitation and hygiene, improving water quality, increasing water – use efficiency, implementing integrated water resources management, and protecting and restoring water-related eco-systems, and progress has been registered; thus between 2000 and 2020 the access to improved drinking water, sanitation facilities and handwashing facilities with soap and water increased to from 82% to 90%, 59% to 68% and 19% to 60 percent, respectively. Even so, WU of VNs has to put in efforts to address challenges like: Inequities in access to WASH services, Water Pollution and Water Scarcity.

7. **AFFORDABLE & CLEAN ENERGY (PSDG:7):** This Goal aims to ensure access to affordable, reliable, sustainable, and modern energy for all by 2050. Targets and indicators already stands set. The progress between 2010 and 2020 also stands measured. Thus the access to electricity, renewable energy and energy efficiency stands increased from 83% to 90%, 21% to 26% and an annual increase of 2.3%, respectively. Yet WU of VNs has to resolves persistent Challenges related to **energy access gaps** (789 million people still lack access to electricity, and 2.8 billion people still rely on polluting fuels for cooking), slow growth of renewable energy and for at least doubling the global rate of growth of energy efficiency.
8. **DECENT WORK AND ECONOMIC GROWTH (PSDG: 8):** For the purpose, multi dimensional targets have been set such as per capita economic growth with at least 7% growth in GDP in least developed countries; achieving higher levels of economic productivity through technological upgratation and innovation; decent job creation & entrepreneurship; achieving full and productive employment and decent work for all women and men, including young people and persons with disabilities; reducing the proportion of youth not in employment, education, or training; protecting labor rights and promoting safe and secure working environments for all workers; strengthening the capacity of domestic financial institutions; increasing access to financial services for; and, implementing policies for progressive and sustainable tourism so as to enable creation of more jobs and promotion of local culture and products. Progress too have been registered in almost above spheres but significant challenges persist which have to be addressed by the WU of VNs. Inequalities in income, widespread informal employment, and unemployment in youth remains high consequently quite sizable number of young people are found struggling for decent jobs/works.
9. **INDUSTRY, INNOVATION & INFRASTRUTURE (PSDG:9):** In as many as 8 fields, targets were reapproved by the expert group along with the determined indicators. These targets relate to: (a) developing of quality infrastructure, including regional and transborder infrastructure to support economic development and human well being; (b) promoting inclusive industrialization in order to increase industry's share in employment and GDP; (c) increasing access to financial services

for small-scale industrial and other enterprises; (d) upgrading infrastructure and retrofit industries; (e) enhancing scientific research and innovation, upgrading technological capabilities of industrial sectors in all countries and encouraging innovation and entrepreneurship; (f) facilitating progressive and sustainable infrastructure development in developing and least developed countries through enhanced financial, technological, and technical support; (g) supporting domestic technology development, research, and innovation in developing and least developed countries; and, (h) increasing significantly access to information and communication technology and strive to provide universal and affordable access to internet. Progress has been registered in these targets, but it has limited to 3 areas only, namely, in matters of access to electricity, the number of internet users and investments in research and development. Significant gaps are still observed in infrastructure, industrialization and innovations. So, continued effort are needed for registering meaningful progress in almost all the targeted areas.

10. **Attaining Progressively Reduced Inequalities (PSDG:10):** This Goal aims to reduce inequalities within and among countries by 2050 and for which as many as 8 targets and 8 indicators were set by UN which the expert group of WU of VNs, do not propose to refine/change, as the progress has been only on two counts. One, some countries have implemented policies to reduce income inequality and two, some efforts have been made to promote social inclusion through education and employment programmes hence challenges persist in respect to (i) Persistent Inequalities; (ii) Discrimination remains significant particularly for marginalized groups; and (iii) migration remains a complex issue with many migrants facing vulnerabilities and challenges.

11. **Progressively Sustainable Cities & Communities [PSDG: 11]:** It aims to make cities and human settlements inclusive, safe, resilient, and progressively sustainable by 2050. Accordingly targets and appropriate indicators for (i) Construction of safe and affordable housing; (ii) transportation; (iii) Urbanization; (iv) protecting Cultural and natural heritage; (v) reducing environmental impact of cities; (vi) reducing the number of deaths and number of people affected by disasters; and (vii) supporting least developed countries in progressively sustainable and resilient building, have been set. However, it is only at two

fronts, namely, Urban Planning and Transportation some progress has so far been witnessed. Therefore, continued efforts are needed in general, and for Urbanization, and reducing inequalities among the people living in informal settlements or lacking success to basic services, in particular. Further, efforts are needed to reduce the risk of disasters and promote progressively sustainable urban development.

12. **PROGRESSIVELY RESPONSIBLE CONSUMPTION & PRODUCTION (PSDG:12):** It focusses on ensuring progressively sustainable consumption and production patterns by 2050. For this purpose targets and indicators have been set for: (i) implementing consumption and production frameworks (two of 10-years each), (ii) management and efficient use of natural resources; (iii) reduction in waste generation; (iv) reduction in food waste; (v) i0mplementing procurement practices in accordance with national policies and priorities; (vi) rationalizing inefficient fossil-fuel subsidies; (vii) encouraging companies to adopt sustainable practices; (viii) promoting public procurement practices; and supporting developing and least developed countries. While some progress has been attained in sustainable consumption and production, but major areas have yet not been touched. Hence, a lot of efforts on the part of WU of VNs are needed particularly for reduction of: (i) over consumption; (ii) waste generation; and, (iii) fossil fuel subsidies.

13. **CLIMATE ACTION (PSDG:13):** It aims to take urgent action for combating climate change and its impacts by achieving the four targets: (a) strengthening resilience and adaptive capacity to climate related hazards and natural disasters in all countries; (b) integrating climate change measures in to national policies, strategies and planning; (c) improving education, awareness-raising and human and institutional capacity on climate change mitigation, adaptation, impact reduction, and early warning; (d) implementing the commitment undertaken by developed-country-parties to mobilize \$100 billion annually for climate finance; and (e) a similar commitment could be attempted for least developed countries. Progress has been made towards securing NDCs (Nationally Determined Contributions) and other commitment for funds for climate action. This aside, Renewal Energy capacity has increased, with solar and wind energy becoming increasingly cost-competitive with fossil fuel. Even

so, much remains to be done for : (a) filling up Emissions Gaps; (b) managing the impacts of climate changes; and (c) for filling up climate finance gaps.

14. **LIFE BELOW WATER (PSDG:14):** Conserving and sustainably using the world's oceans, seas, and marine resources for progressively sustainable development upto 2050 is the prime objective of this PSDG14. For attaining this, several targets have been finalized such as: (i) reducing marine pollution; (ii) protecting and restoring marine eco-systems; (iii) reducing overfishing; (iv) conserving marine biodiversity at least by 20 percent; (v) prompting tourism; (vi) eliminating illegal fishing; (vii) increasing scientific knowledge, develop research capacity, and transfer marine technology; and, (viii) improving conservation and management of fisheries. Progress has so far been achieved in respect to the protected marine areas; adoption of sustainable fishing practices and in research and development in marine technology. But, WU of VNs needs to put in efforts on **'Over Fishing'; 'Marine Pollution and Impect on Marine Eco-systems & Climate Change.**

15. **Life on Land (PSDG:15):** Protecting, restoring, and promoting progressively sustainable use of terrestrial ecosystems, forests, and bio-diversity by 2050 are some purpose of this PSDG:15. Number of targets have been finalized along with required indicators by the expert group. Major targets being: (i) promoting of sustainable forest management, reforestation, afforestation, and restoration; (ii) combating desertification, restoring degraded land and soil; (iii) ensuring conservation of mountain ecosystems; (iv) protecting and preventing the extinction of threatened species, including endangered species of fauna and flora; (v) promoting fair and equitable sharing of benefits arising from the utilization of genetic resources; (vi) taking urgent action to end poaching and trafficking; and (vii) integrating ecosystem and biodiversity values in to national planning, development processes and poverty reduction strategies. As against these targets, progress had only been on three scores, namely, increase in the proportion of terrestrial ecosystems conserved, sustainable forest management practices and in combating desertification and restoring degraded land, rest remains to be done vigorously in case of deforestation, biodiversity loss, and poaching and trafficking.

16. **PROGRESSIVE PEACE, JUSTICE & STRONG INSTITUTIONS FOR ALL (PSDG: 16):** Whereas we have already discussed about Peace in the beginning of this chapter, yet we would like to have a distinct PSDG:16 focusing on this subject. Under this orbit of development we would like that WU of VNs must focus on promoting peaceful and inclusive societies and on access to justice for all and building effective, accountable, financially strong and inclusive institutions at all levels with a view to: (i) reduce violence and related death rates; (ii) end abuse and exploitation/ torture of children; (iii) promoting the rule of law at the national and international levels and ensuring equal justice for all; (iv) ensuring inclusive and participatory decision-making; and, (v) ensuring public assess to information and protecting fundamental freedoms. No doubt, progress has been registered on the front of reducing violence and improving access to justice, yet significant challenges exist in respect to conflicts and violence, inequality and discriminations, corruption, lack of transparency and limited access to information. But in years ahead much wonderful progress is possible in general and with the assistance of technological innovations and through seeking international cooperation.

17. **PROGRESSIVE PARTNERSHIPS FOR ACCOMPLISHING GOALS (PSDG:17):** Without disturbing the sequence, the expert group also recommended to the Board of Governors of the newly created WU of VNs to implement this SGD 17, of course in the up to the extended time frame of 2050. Primarily, this PSDG:17 stressed on two aspects. **One,** strengthening of the 'means' employed for implementing its variegated actions and, **two,** on revitalizing the global partnerships with different countries/global, regional, public-private institutions/civil society partnerships. As part of this, various targets have been set up so as to include finance, technology, domestic resource mobilization, improving domentic capacity for tax and other revenue collection, enhancing the benefits of international trade for developing countries, promoting an universal rule-based, open and non-discriminatory and equitable multilateral trading system, enhancing global macro-economic stability, and data, monitoring and accountability corresponding to these targets indicators too have been laid down. But saving the areas of mobilizing of financial resources, promoting

technology transfer, and strengthening capacity building, not much has so far been attained due to insufficient funding, inequitable trade, limited technology transfer, weak capacity building and inadequate data and monitoring. The ample opportunities however, exist for innovative financing mechanisms, utilization of digital technologies, and for expanding global partnerships. The WU of VNs must exploit to its maxima for implementing the agenda set under this PSDG17.

Annexure on: "CAPRICIOUS GLOBAL EDUCATION"

Global Education is defined as **"the pursuit of knowledge, ideas and understanding by people in diverse cultures, identies locations and backgrounds."** And, as per UNESCO global education is to enable each generation peace through their own efforts. Before we take up the issue pertaining to integration, let us first elaborate the phrases 'Ethics', 'Human Values' and 'Psychology Rules for Conduct'.

SUBJECTS TO BE INTEGRATED

(a) Ethics

There are several schools of thought on 'ethics'. On this basis the Ethics could be descriptive, normative, deontological ethics (duty ethics), consequentialist ethics (ethical correctness of an action on the basis foreseeable consequences), virtue ethics, meta ethics and applied ethics. We here are most concerned with normative ethics, and machine and applied ethics. **In normative, 'Ethics'** is defined as the analysis of human actions from the perspective of **"good"** and **"evil"** or of **"morally correct"** and **"morally wrong"**. Machine ethics attempts to answer the question: What would it take to build an ethical AI that could make moral decisions? The main difference between human making moral decisions and machine making moral decisions is that machines do not have **"phenomenology"** or **"feelings"** in the same way as human do. And, it is for philosophical convenience, we assume our AI is embedded in a humanoid robot and can act in much the same way as a human.

(b) Human Values

It refers to the basic inherent moral inclinations towards kindness, honesty, loyalty, love, peace, sympathy, truth etc underpinning the fundamental goodness of human beings and society at large. They are the values that human being cherishes or hold in common consciously and otherwise, in most of the places and times and practice them. Human values help in understanding the attitudes, motivation and behaviours and also influences our perception of the world around us. They enable the interpretation of "right and wrong" and provide the ways to understand individuals and organizations. The principal human values are discussed in brief as under:

1. **Love and Compassion:** Love manifests in sincere care of others, kindness, empathy and compassion for all. True unconditional love leads to compassion. It may be inoperation in human acts of generosity, mercy and charity.
2. **Peace:** Peace contains values like equality, humility, optimism, patience, self-confidence, self-control, self-esteem etc. Its scope includes peace at the level of individual, society and the world.
3. **Truth:** Truth is external and unchanging , as it deals with ultimate and unchanging reality. It is marked with values like accuracy, fairness, honesty, sincerity, justice, fearlessness, integrity, quest for knowledge, determination, etc. In professional life, the simplest manifestation of truth is in sincerity that can be seen in terms of commitment to work.
4. **Non-Violence:** It refers to restraint from consciously doing any harm through one's thoughts, speech or action to any entity, living or non-living.

Non-violence demands abstinence from hatred and nurturing love and compassion for all beings.

5. **Righteousness:** It is the backbone of core human values as it involves conduct of life and action by practicing propriety and decorum at very stage. It covers ethical guidelines, ethical behaviour and moral values.
6. **Renunciation:** It connotes caring attitude towards all living beings without any selfish motives. It is seen in austerity, self-control and selflessness of a person.
7. **Service:** It is an action performed out of love. It also stands for compassion and sacrifice for others. The value of service demands equanimity without any conditions or discrimination based on caste, creed, race, region and religion.
8. **Peaceful Co-existence:** It describes cohesive and coherent relationships. It contains psychological and social values such as benevolence, compassion, consideration, morality, forgiveness, brotherhood, equality, perseverance, respects for others, environmental awareness, etc.
9. **Discipline:** It indicates regulated values followed by the individual for all beings. It contains value like regulation, direction, order etc.[3]

   In the context of Human Values & Ethics, the Human Values Foundation, UK categorically observed that the ideal age for formally imparting education in human values is when the children are of 5 to 12 years of age i.e., when they are being imparted their primary level education. However, if it is not done in any country/community/society for any reason, then the same could be taken up either of the stage when they are getting middle level, secondary level or higher level of education *via* appropriate Teaching Manual-full of tips, practical guidance, and expert advice.

Also, the higher-level learning in regard ethics and human values could be demonstrated *via* course curriculum designs, teaching methods, extracurricular activities, emphasis on value-based education in teachers training and school culture followed for graduation or higher level of education.

(c) Psychology Rules that Governs Good Conduct of People

The important psychology rules which govern the good conduct of people are as under:

A. Social Psychology Rules

1. Reciprocity Rule: People tend to reciprocate kindness and generosity.
2. Social Norms Rule: People follow norms and expectations of their social group.
3. Authority Rule: People tend to obey authority figures.
4. Liking Rule: People are more likely to help those they like.
5. Consistency Rule: People prefer to act consistently with their previous actions.

B. Moral Psychology Rules

1. Golden Rule: Treating others as you would like to be treated.

2. Empathy Rule: People who empathise with others are more likely to act morally.
3. Fairness Rule: People prefer fairness and justice.
4. Guilt Rule: Feelings of guilt can motivate moral behaviour.
5. Self Interest Rule- People's self-interest can motivate moral behaviour.

C. Cognitive Psychology Rules

1. Cognitive Dissonance Rule: People seek consistency between thoughts and action.
2. Self Perception Rule: People's self image influences their behaviour.
3. Availability Heuristic Rule: People overestimate the importance of vivid information.
4. Hindsight Bias Rule: People tend to believe, after an event, that they would have predicted it.
5. Framing Effect Rule: People's decisions are influenced by how information is presented.

D. Emotional Intelligence Rules

1. Emotional Regulation Rule: People who manage their emotions effectively act more morally.
2. Empathy Rule: People who empathize into anothers act more morally.
3. Self-Awareness Rule: People who understand themselves act more morally.
4. Motivation Rule: People's motivations influence their moral behaviour.
5. Relationship Rule: People's relationships influence their moral behaviour.

E. Developmental Psychology Rules

1. Moral Developmental Rule: People progress through stages of moral development.
2. Social Learning Rule: People learn moral behaviour through observation and initiation.
3. Attachment Rule: People's attachment styles influence their moral behaviour
4. Identity Rule: People's sense of identity influence their moral behaviour.
5. Culture Rule: Cultural norms and values influence moral behaviour.

F. Neuro Science Rules

1. Reward System Rule: The brain's reward system motivates moral behaviour.
2. Stress Response Rule: Chronic stress impairs moral decision making.
3. Mirror Neurons Rule: Mirror neurons facilitate empathy and moral behaviour.
4. Prefrontal Cortex Rule: The prefrontal cortex regulates moral decision making.
5. Neuroplasticity Rule: The brains ability to reorganize influences moral behaviour.

The above-mentioned Psychology Rules explain as to why people engage in good conduct and provide insights for promoting moral behaviour.

II. INTEGRATING HUMAN VALUES, ETHICS & PSYCYOLOGY RULES OF CONDUCT INTO GLOBAL EDUCATION

World Union of Visionary Nations' Holistic Model: It would foster a more compassionate, responsible and socially conscious global citizenry. Elaborating this, we can say that this modal would:

- Promote social – emotional learning;
- Foster Empathy, compassion, and understanding;
- Develop critical thinking and moral reasoning;
- Encourage responsible decision making; and
- Enhance global citizenship and cultural competence.

Such citizen in their turn will be respecting the following human values, ethical considerations, and psychology rules of conduct too:

(a) Human Values:

1. Diversity and inclusiveness;
2. Empathy and compassion;
3. Integrity and honesty;
4. Responsibility and accountability;
5. Critical thinking and inquiry;
6. Creativity and innovation;
7. Environmental sustainability;
8. Social justice, fairness and equality;
9. Global citizenship and cultural awareness; and
10. Emotional intelligence and well being.

(b) Ethical Considerations

1. Human Rights based approach as included in Universal Declaration of Human Rights (UDHR)
2. Care-Ethics;
3. Virtue-Ethics;
4. Social Contract Theory;
5. World Union for Visionary Nations' Progressive Sustainable Development Goals; and
6. World Union for Visionary Nations' four pillars of learning:
   - Learning to know;
   - Learning to do;
   - Learning to live together; and
   - Learning to Be.

(c) Psychology Rules of Conduct

1. Social norms theory;
2. Emotional Intelligence framework;

3. Moral Development Theory; and
4. Empathy altruism hypothesis.

III. STRATEGIES FOR INTEGRATION

1. Incorporate Value based education.
2. Integrate Ethics and moral education.
3. Teach Social-emotional learning skills.
4. Encourage service learning of community engagement
5. Foster global citizenship education.

IV. CURRICULUM DEVELOMENT FOR DIFFERENT LEVELS OF EDUCATION

While courses on STEM and SKILLS-ORIENTED may be included at Secondary, Higher Secondary, Graduation and Higher Studies level (Post-Graduate and above) and curriculum development of the prescribed courses may be developed as per the expertise expected. We are now confining our discussion in respect to integrated courses related ethics, values and code of conduct. But surely from the beginning and upto Higher Studies Level. There are four broad aspects related to curriculum development in so far as these levels of education is concerned: (a) Integrating human values and psychology rules into existing subjects e.g. social studies, literature; (b) developing stand alone courses e.g. Ethics, Moral Education; (c) Incorporating Case Studies and real-world examples; and (d) encouraging critical thinking and reflection. Accordingly, there shall be **two** broad categories of courses/topics in this area. **One** purely theoretical/conceptual Courses, and **two** Applied courses/ topics. Upto post-graduate level the combination of both types be included. Thus the focus areas of inclusion in curriculum development at different levels of education would be as thus in brief.

(a) Primary Level (Age 5-11)

1. Values-based education integrated into subjects like social studies, language and arts.
2. Cultural Awareness and diversity.
3. Focus on emotional intelligence, empathy and social skills.
4. Environment education.
5. Basic human rights and responsibilities.
6. Storytelling and role-playing to teach values and ethics.
7. Single decision-making and problem-solving exercises.

Example Topics:

- Respect for others.
- Honesty and Integrity.
- Sharing and Caring.
- Emotional Awareness.
- Basic Moral Principles.

(b) Middle Level (Age 12-14)

1. Ethics and Moral Education as a separate subject.
2. Case studies and group discussions on real life scenarios.

3. Developing Critical Thinking and decision-making skills.
4. Introduction to diverse cultures and global issues.

Example Topics

- Friendship and relationships.
- Bullying and Conflict resolution.
- Environmental responsibility.
- Basic Human Rights.

(c) Secondary Level (Age 15-18)

1. In-depth ethics and moral philosophy courses.
2. Analysis of Complex issues and global challenges.
3. Developing leadership and community service skills.
4. Integration with subjects like history, economics and politics.
5. Human Rights and Social Justice.
6. Environmental Sustainability and conservation.

Examples of Topics

- Identity and self-awareness.
- Social Justice and Activism.
- Media literacy and critical thinking.
- Global citizenship and responsibility.
- Advanced moral principles.

(d) Graduate Level (age 19-22)

1. Specialized courses on Ethics, Moral Philosophy and Social Responsibility.
2. Emotional Intelligence and wellbeing.
3. In-depth analysis of global issues and case studies.
4. Human rights and international law.
5. Developing research and critical thinking skills.
6. Leadership and social responsibility.
7. Integration with subjects like business studies, law, healthcare, etc

Illustrative examples

- Advanced Moral theories and frameworks.
- Global governance and international relations.
- Business ethics and corporate social responsibility
- Health Ethics and Medical decision making.
- Environmental Sustainability.

(e) Higher Studies Level (Post-graduate and above)

1. Advanced Research and specialization in Ethics and Moral Philosophy.
2. Interdisciplinary approaches integrating psychology, sociology and philosophy.
3. Focus on applied ethics in various fields e.g. Bio-ethics, environmental ethics.
4. Development of leadership and policy making skills.

Illustrative Topics

- Advanced Moral Theories and critiques.
- Global Ethics and human rights.
- Ethics in Science and Technology.
- Organizational Ethics and Leadership.
- Policy making and social change.

V. KEY CONSIDERATIONS ACROSS ALL LEVELS OF EDUCATION

1. Age-appropriate content and pedagogy.
2. Integration with existing subjects and curriculum.
3. Teacher Training and Support.
4. Community Involvement and Partnerships.
5. Continuous Evaluation and Improvement.

(a) Teaching methods

1. Experintial learning.
2. Project based learning.
3. Service learning.
4. Storytelling and narrative pedagogy.
5. Debate and discussion.

(b) Assessment and evolution

1. Reflective journals and self-assessment.
2. Peer review and feedback.
3. Project based evalution.
4. Service-learning reflection papers.
5. Standardized Tests (critical thinking and problem solving).

(c) Teacher training and support

1. Professional Development workshops.
2. Mentorships programs.
3. Collaborative planning and teaching.

(d) Community Engagements and partnerships

1. Local community partnerships.
2. Global networking and collaborations.
3. Service-learning projects.
4. Parent and Community involvement.
5. Alumni engagement and mentorship.

(e) Monitoring and evalution

1. Regular curriculum reviews.
2. Student and Teacher Feedback.
3. Community engagement and partnership evaluation.
4. Alumni tracking and outcomes assessment.
5. Continuous improvement and adaptation.

VI. MERGING THIS CURRICULUM WITH THE REGULAR CURRICULUM OF EDUCATION

- Primary Level curriculum.
- Middle Level curriculum.
- Secondary and higher secondary level curriculum.
- Graduation level curriculum.
- Post-Graduation and advanced level higher education/specialized curriculums.

VII. COMPETITIVE EXAMINIATIONS

While for persuing higher studies large number of Competitive Examinations are conducted all over the world such as SAT (Scholastic Aptitude Test) – USA; ACT (American College Testing) – USA; GRE (Graduate Record Examinations) – USA; GMAT (Graduate Management Admission Test) – USA; LSAT (Law School Admission Test)-USA; MCAT (Medical College Admission Test) – USA; TOEFL (Test of English as a Foreign Language) – USA; IELTS (Inter-national English Language Testing System) – UK/Australia/New Zealand; A-Level (Advanced Level) UK; IB Diploma (International Baccalaureate Diploma)- Switzerland; Gaokao (National College Entrance Examination) China; JEE (Joint Entrance Examination) India; and NEET (National Eligibility Cum Entrance Test) – India. Likewise, quite a sizeable number of competitive examinations are held for administrative services both at centre and state levels. For example, UPSC (Union Public Service Commission – India) conducts examination for recruitment at central level IAS, IPS, IFS, etc. In USA CSE (Civil Service Examination) is conducted for Federal Government Jobs. Federal Civil Service Commission conducts FCSC examination in Pakistan. And in Canada, Australia and several other countries, PSC (Public Service Commissions of respective country) is being conducted for recruitment at Central level. Similarly for filling up administrative vacancies State PSCs State Public Service Commissions like the of UPSC, MPSC, TNPSC, etc) hold competitive examinations in India. In USA (e.g. California, New York). State Civil Service Examination is held. Provincial Civil Service Commission and State Public Sector Commission conducts identical examinations in Pakistan and Australia, respectively.

The point that we wish to emphasize is: Can't we also include a course on 'Ethics, Valves and Conduct' in all of these competitive examinations? Well the expert Group on 'Global Education' may critically examine it and can come out with an illustrative MODEL syllabus and an illustrative **examination** PAPER on this course covering both conceptual questions and case study base questions. We are of the considered opinion that it must be done under the situations we are living today.

VIII. PROFESSIONALS, CORPORATE EXECUTIVES & POLITICIANS

Of course with a gap of 3-5 years, either in the form of a Training Programme or Workshop of 1 to 3 days too should be organized for all professionals, corporate executives and politicians, irrespective of the Position they might be holding, wherein the Real Case Studies and situational aspects covering ethical, value and conduct-based be discussed along with the actual results and be concluded as to how change in value and conduct-based behaviour might have resulted for good and progress of the concerned community and *vice-a-versa*.

ENDNOTES

1. Absence of conflict means a state of being free from war, violence, or disturbance. Inner Calm include a feeling of Tranquity, Serenity, and Mental calmness. And 'Harmony' states a state of mutual understanding, respect and cooperation.
2. 'Inclusive Peace' is a state where everyone, regardless of their background, culture or identity, feels safe, respected and valued. Universal Harmony is a global state of peace, where all individuals and communities coexist in mutual respect, understanding and cooperation. And, 'Social Justice' depicts a state where, everyone has equal access to resources, opportunities, and human rights.
3. See, please, Hand book title, "Human Values & Professional Ethics", Guru Nanak Dev University, Amritsar, India. Also, see, please, "Handbook for Human Values & Ethics," Sri Manakulo Vinaygar Engineering College, Puducherry, 60517; "Human Values Foundation" 2009, Registered office; The Coach House, Salisbury Road, Horshan West Succeyax RHS 30A, UK; Website: www.https://humanvaluesfoundation.com

CHAPTER - 10

ACCOMPANIER STRATEGY OF WORLD UNION OF VISIONARY NATIONS (WUVN)

Alongside the PSDG17, the World Union of Visionary Nations shall also adopt an **Ideal Model of Governance with Global Applicability with the aid of** expert group established for the purpose. In order to effectively attain the variegated Goals. The outlines of this Ideal Model are as given hereunder.

1. **Core Principles:**
    1. Transparency
    2. Accountability
    3. Participation
    4. Inclusivity
    5. Equity
    6. Sustainability
    7. Human Rights
    8. Rule of Law
2. **Structural Components:**
    1. Decentralized Decision Making.
    2. Representative and Participatory Democracy.
    3. Independent Judiciary.
    4. Free and Independent Media.
    5. Civil Society Engagement
    6. International Cooperation and Collaborations.

3. **Key Institutions:**
    1. Local Governance Councils.
    2. National Parliamentary Assembly.
    3. Global Parliamentary Assembly.
    4. International Court of Justice.
    5. Human Rights Commission.
    6. Environmental Protection Agency.
    7. Economic Development Agency.
4. **Decision-making Processes:**
    1. Consensus Based Decision Making.
    2. Majority Voting with Minority Protection.
    3. Public Consultations and Referendums.
    4. Expert Advisory Committees.
    5. Transparency and Accountability Mechanisms.
5. **Accountability Mechanisms:**
    1. Independent Auditing and Evaluation.
    2. Whistleblower Protection.
    3. Anti-Corruption Agencies.
    4. Public Access to Information.
    5. Media freedom and investigative journalism.
6. **Participatory Mechanisms:**
    1. Citizen Engagement Platforms.
    2. Public Hearings and Town Hall Meetings.
    3. Representative Sampling and deliberative polling.
    4. Online participatory budgeting.
    5. Social Media Engagement.
7. **Global Cooperation:**
    1. International Treaties and Agreements.
    2. Global Economic Cooperation.
    3. Environmental Agreements.
    4. Human Rights Conventions.
    5. Peacekeeping and Conflict Resolution.

8. Technological Integration:

1. Blockchain-based Transparency and of Accountability.
2. Artificial Intelligence for Data Analysis.
3. Digital Participation Platforms.
4. Cybersecurity Measures.
5. Data Driven Decision Making.

9. Education & Capacity Building:

1. Civic Education and Critical Thinking.
2. Leadership Development Programs.
3. Public Administration Training.
4. International Exchange Programs.
5. Capacity Building for Marginalized Group.

10. Monitoring and Evaluation:

1. Regular Performance Assessments.
2. Citizen Satisfaction Surveys.
3. Independent Evaluations.
4. International Peer Review.
5. Continuous Improvement and Adaptation.

11. Challenges and Mitigation Strategies:

1. Addressing Power Imbalances.
2. Managing Conflicts of Interest.
3. Ensuring Inclusivity and Diversity.
4. Balancing Individual and Collective Rights.
5. Adapting to Emerging Global Challenges.

IMPLEMENTATION ROADMAP

1. **SHORT TERM (0-5 years):** Establish local governance councils, national parliamentary assemblies and global parliamentary assemblies.
2. **MEDIUM TERM (5-10 years):** Develop international cooperation mechanisms, establish independent judiciary, and implement participatory mechanisms.

3. **LONG TERM (10-20 years or more):** Achieve full decentralization, ensure global cooperation and integrate technology.

Thus the **Ideal Model of Governance prioritizes transparency, accountability, participation and inclusivity ensuring equitable decision-making and progressive sustainable development.**

ANOTHER STUMBLING BLOCK IS INCREASING NUMBER OF CONFLICTS THAT IS ETCHING THE PROGRESSIVE DEVELOPMENT OF THE WORLD

Aside absence of global participatory governance, the world is currently experiencing a surge in conflicts, with the highest number of countries involved in conflicts since World War II. There are 56 ongoing conflicts globally with 92 countries involved in conflicts outside their borders. These conflicts have resulted in an unprecedented humanitarian needs, with upto 300 million people requiring aid in 2024. And, global economic impact of violence has gone up and reached to $19.1 Trillion in 2023.

GLOBAL CONFLICTS

Same of the most pressing ongoing global conflicts are:

- **Gaza Conflict:** The conflicts in Gaza has escalated, resulting in over 42,000 deaths and 99,000 injuries. The situation is dire, with 1.9 million people forced to leave their homes, and a risk of famine looming.
- **South Sudanese Conflict:** Fighting between the Sudanese army and the **Rapid Support Forces** has led to enormous humanitarian crisis with over 18,000 deaths and 33,000 injuries, and 12 million people displaced.
- **Ukraine-Russia Conflict or Russo-Ukrainian War:** Started in 2014 between Russia and Ukraine. The conflict has intensified with attacks on civilians and infrastructure leaving 14.6 million people in need of humanitarian assistance.
- **Syrian Civil War:** It is a conflict between Syrian Govt. and various opposition groups, including extremist organizations like ISIS. The war has entered its 14th year, with 70 per cent of Syrians in need of humanitarian aid. The situation is exacerbated by a widespread economic crisis and food shortages.

- **Democratic Republic of Congo Conflict:** The country faces one of the world's most protracted crises, caused by armed conflict, economic crisis, climate shocks, and disease epidemics. Humanitarian needs are estimated at 25.4 million people, the highest of any country globally.
- **Yemen Conflict:** It is a conflict between the Yemeni govt. and Houthi rebels with involvement from regional powers like Saudi Arabia and Iran. The conflicts has pushed the economy to the verge of collapse, with a rising risk of famine and displacement.
- **Myanmar Conflict:** Started in 1948, the situation has deteriorated since the military coup in Feb 2021, with renewed clashes between armed groups and the Government. It has resulted in 28,672 to 180,000 cumulative fatalities with 3065 reported in 2023.
- **Nigerian Conflict:** The country saw a coup in July 2024, with rising violence and displacement. It involves the Nigerian Govt. Boko Haram insurgents, and other extremist groups.
- **Afghanistan Conflict:** A decades – long conflict involving the Afghan Government, Taliban insurgents and international forces.
- **Iraq Conflict:** Ongoing violence involving the Iraqi Government, extremist group, like ISIS, and Kurdish Separatists.
- **Libyan Conflict:** A conflict between the **Libyan Government** and various militias, with involvement from regional powers.
- **Central African Republic Conflict:** A conflict between the CAR Govt. and various rebel groups fueled by ethnic and political tensions.
- **Indian Kashmir Conflict:** A long standing conflict between India and Pakistan over the disputed region of Kashmir. Philippine conflict. A Conflict between the Philippine govt and various rebel groups, including the **New People's Army.**
- **Philippine's Conflict:** A conflict between the Philippine Govt. and various rebel groups, including the New People's Army
- **Mali Conflict:** Ongoing violence involving the **Malian Government** and various extremist groups, including **Al-Qaeda** in the **Islamic Magheb.**
- **Burkina Faso Conflict:** A conflict between **Burkinabe Govt.** and various extremist groups, including **Al-Qaeda** in the **Islamic Maghreb.**

- **Guinea – Bissau Conflict:** A conflict between the Guinea – Bissau Govt. and various rebel groups.
- **Sierra Leone conflict:** Ongoing violence involving the **Sierra Leonean Govt.** and various rebel groups.
- **Cote d'l voire Conflict:** A conflict between the **Ivorian Govt.** and various rebel groups.
- **Liberia Conflict:** Ongoing violence involving **Liberian Govt.** and various rebel groups.
- **Ethiopia Conflict:** A Conflict between the **Ethiopian Government** and various rebel groups, fueled by ethnic and political tensions.
- **Some important Skirmishes and clashes (fewer than 100 deaths in current and previous years)**
  - Albania-Greece Border Dispute.
  - Bosnia and Herzegovina-Serbia Border Dispute.
  - Croatia-Slovenia Border Dispute.
  - Ecuador-Colombia Border Dispute.
  - Georgia-Russia Border Dispute.
  - Guyana-Venezuela Border Dispute.
  - Kosovo-Serbia Border Dispute.
- **Somali conflict:** Ongoing violence involving the **Somali Govt.,** extremist groups like **Al-Sha baab**, and international forces.
- **Colombian Conflict:** A conflict between the **Colombian Govt.** and various rebel groups including **FARC** and **ELN.**
- **CAMEROON CONFLICT:** A Conflict between the **Cameroonian Govt.** and separatist groups in the **Anglophone** region.
- **Chad Conflict:** Ongoing violence involving the **Chadian Government** and various rebel groups.
- **Turkey-PKK Conflict:** A long standing conflict between **Turkey** and the **Kurdistan Workers' Party (PKK).**
- **Uzbekistan Conflict:** Ongoing violence involving the **Uzbek Govt.** and various extremist groups.

REGIONAL CONFLICTS & KEY TRINDS

1. **Middle East or North Africa:** This region has the highest number of armed conflicts, with over 45 ongoing conflicts with over 45 countries such as **Syria, Yemen, Libya and Iraq.**

2. **Africa:** There are over 35 armed conflicts in Africa, with countries such as the **Democratic Republic of Congo, South Sudan,** and **Somalia** being affected.
3. **Asia:** The region is experiencing 21 armed conflicts, with countries as **Afghanistan, India** and **the Philippines** being impacted.
4. **Europe:** There are 7 ongoing armed conflicts in **Europe,** including that of **Ukraine.**
5. **Latin America:** The region has 6 ongoing armed conflicts, with countries such as **Mexico** and **Colombia** being affected.

KEY TRENDS

- The number of conflict-related deaths has increased, with **1,62,000 deaths** recorded in 2023.
- The global economic impact of violence has also increased, with an estimated **$ 19.1 Trillion in losses in 2023.**
- The use of asymmetric warfare technology, such as drones, has become more prevalent, making it easier for non-state groups to compete in conflicts.

The above being the petrifying picture of armed conflicts/disputes spread over to 92 countries, the task of resolving these by the created expert group for conflicts resolutions obviously become strenuous in view of it getting enlarged spontaneously. The major conflicts/Disputes, stands enumerated as above. It should develop an **inner strategy,** which may have different features for amicably resolving these over a stipulated period dividing these into major and minor violences. The Expert Group is to remain open for employing all kinds of plans, manoeuvers and campaign for solving the issues involved in each conflict among countries involved. And, multifaceted approach may be needed to achieve success. Even so, the **standard framework** for conflict resolution could be phased as thus:

I. **Pre-Negotiation Phase:**

(a) Ceasefire agreements;

(b) Confidence Building; and

(c) International Mediation.

II. **Negotiation Phase:**

1. Direct talks;

2. Issue - based Negotiations, and,
3. Creative Solutions.

III. Agreement Phase:

1. **Developing Framework Agreements** outlining the principles and parameters of a comprehensive peace agreement.
2. Detailed Negotiations on Specific Aspects of the Agreement.
3. Securing International Guarantees.

IV. Implementation Phase:

1. Monitoring Mechanisms.
2. Gradual Implementation.
3. Economic Support- such as aid or investments, to help parties rebuild and stabilize

V. Post Conflict Phase:

1. Reconciliation Efforts.
2. Institution – Building.
3. Long-term development.

KEY PRINCIPLES

While following the multiphased above framework for resolving conflicts, the undermentioned major principles be taken care of:

1. Mutual Recognition;
2. Non-Violence;
3. Inclusivity;
4. Flexibility; and,
5. International support.

We trust that if the expert group will adhere to above principles and frame, then even the most complex conflicts shall stand resolved.

CHAPTER – 11

CURRENT SCENARIO & WORLD UNION OF VISIONARY NATIONS

NAVIGATING FOR COUPLE OF MINUTES: RECENT NEWS *VIA* VARIEGATED MEDIA AS GIVEN ILLUSTRATIVELY

1. "The US department of state has updated eligibility requirements for interview waiver appointments (referred to as dropbox appointments).... Under the revised rules, dropbox is available only to applicants renewing a visa in the same non-immigrant category that has expired within past 12 months."[1]

2. "The Trump administration is looking at banning citizens of 43 countries from travelling to the United States.... A draft list developed by diplomatic and security officials suggests a **"red"** list of 11 Countries whose citizens would be flatly barred from entering US. These include Afghanistan, Bhutan, Iran, North Korea, Cuba, and Venezuela ... The proposal also included an "**Orange List"** of 10 countries including Russia, Pakistan, Myanmar for which travel would be restricted, and a **"Yellow"** list of 22 countries (Several African Countries, Cambodia) that would be given 60 days to clear up perceived deficiencies."[2]

3. Prime Minister Narendra Modi said... "Differences and disagreements are natural among the neighboring countries just like those in a family, but our efforts are focused on ensuring that these differences do not turn into confrotations. The 21st century is the century of Asia. Good relations between India and China are not just beneficial but also important for global stability and prosperity." ...... On the India-Pakistan conflicts Modi said, "India wants peace but for long terror acts in India and the world have been found to have their origins in Pakistan."......... Modi also expressed optimism on relations with US President Donald Trump and underlined that there are similarities between DOGE and the measures he has taken in India. On Trump's praise for him, Modi said, "It in Trump's magnanimity that he praised me .... Just as it is America First for him, it is India First for me."[3]

4. "Israeli air strikes pounded Gaza and killed more the 400 people, Palestinian health authorities said..... in an onslaught across the enclave that ended weeks of relative calm after talks to secure a permanent ceasefire stalled?"[4]

   Zelensky who arrived to Finland ... to discuss the Nato state's support for Ukraine said "Ukraine's sovereignty is not negotiable and Russia must surrender the territory it has seized."[5]

5. Following two articles also appeared in the Times of India, News Paper, New Delhi, 19 March, 2025, India: (i) One by **Dan Cassino** "Liberty's Getting Trumped in US:" (in student/tourists visas Green Cards, Trump has found an easy way to demonstrate power. The Costs will be borne not just by 'foreigners' but by America itself); (ii) **Two,** by **Xu Felhong,** "India-China can Achieve A Dragon-Elephant Tango...... Next month marks 75 years of diplomatic relations, Chinese ambassador writes that development the biggest shared goal, benefits from synergy between New Delhi and Beijing)."[6]

6. In an article, "WTO: New Tariff likely to Hit Trade in Medium Term", it was observed that: "Increased trade policy uncertainly and prospects of new tariffs could weigh on global trade in the medium-term......"[7]

7. In another article-titled, **"Dogs of war: Russian Rumble Makes Ukraine Top Arms Buyer"**......., "Ukraine has displaced India as the world's largest arms importer in the 2020-24 time frame, with its imports skyrocketing by nearly 100 times compared to 2015-19 due to its ongoing debilitating war with Russia...... India notched up 8.3 percent of global arms imports in 2020-24, driven largely by heightened tensions with China and Pakistan, while Ukraine stood at 8.8% as per as latest data on international transfers released by the Stockholm International Peace Research Institute (SIPRI) on March 10, 2025......Overall, European arms imports grew by 155 percent fueled by fears of Russia's expansionism after invading Ukraine in Feb. 2022 and prevailing uncertainty over the future of US Foreign Policy under the new Trump administration. Pakistan's arms import, incidentally increased by 61 percent between 2015-19 and 2020-24. It was placed fifth in the world ranking, with 81 percent of its weapons coming from China, in yet another indicator of the ever-expanding military collusiveness between India's two hostile neighbours .... New Delhi's increasing ability to design and produces its own weapons."[8]

8. "Listing the revocation of the special status of J&K as one of the steps taken by India to settle the Kashmir issue, foreign minister, S. Jaishankar said if Pakistan returns the "Stolen part" of Kashmir's to India, the matter would be fully resolved." (Stolen part is approximately 78000 sq. km).[9]

9. "China says ready for any "Type of War" after reciprocal tariffs talk."[10]

10. "The most recent United Nations Climate Change Conference, (COP29)/ focused on finance, but it fell short in more ways than one. The contentious negotiations – representatives from several developing countries walked out in protest – defied the odds to produce a commitment the **"Baku Climate Unity Pact"** from developed economies to deliver $300 billion in climate funding annually to their poorer counterparts by 2035...... That is triple the target agreed in 2009 (and reached, for the first time, in 2022) but it is nowhere near the estimated $ 1.3 trillion in annual financing that developing economics will need over this period.......It's only one part of the problem. The reality is that as world leaders clashed in Baku amid unprecedented international tensions, the true battle being waged was the future of **Climate finance and Women's role in it.** Women and Children are 14 times more likely to die in climate-related disasters than men, and women comprise 80 percent of those displaced by extreme weather."[11]

11. On December 9, 2024 India makes Huge Announcement on **New Currency:** The BRICS block created a mock-up currency during the 16th summit in October. Russian President Vladimir Putin proudly displayed the mock-up bill to all the attendees. The currency in question would challenge the US Dollar's hegemony and dim its demand in the global supply mechanism. India is, however, slowly distancing itself from the de-dollarization agenda. India's Foreign Minister **S. Jaishankar** confirmed that **India is not interested in pursuing the de-dollarization agenda.** Jaishankar added that a BRICS currency is not in the works, and India will not stop depending on the US Dollar. To quote him, "There is a personal relationship between PM Modi and Trump. Where the BRICS remarks were concerned, we have said that India has never been for de-dollarization. Rights now there is no proposal to have a BRICS currency. The BRICS do discuss financial transactions. The US is our largest trade partner, we have no interest in weakening the US Dollar at all," said Jai Shankar.[12]

12. In Continuation to above, on March 6, 2025, Vinod Dsouza, further stated that "India officially dismisses BRICS currency, praises the US Dollar." And, speaking at a session titled "India's Rise and Role in the worlds" in London, Jaishankar confirmed that they're not interested in BRICS currency. "I do not think there is any policy on our part to replace the US Dollar. As I said, ….. the dollar as the reserve currency is the source of International economic stability. And, right now, what we want in the world is more economic stability, not less", he said.[13]

    "The death toll from two days of clashes between security forces and loyalists of ousted Syrian President Bashar Assad and revenge killing that followed has risen to more than 600, a war monitoring group said Saturday, making it one of the deadliest acts of violence since **Syria's** conflicts began 14 years ago…." As reported on March 10, 2025 the death toll has increased to more than 1000......, On 11th March as shown in Times of India, Shocking Video Shows Dozen Bodies on Latakia streets, chilling videos from Syria's Latakia show the aftermath of deadly clash. Dozens of bodies lie in the streets as women wail in grief. Reports indicated that most victims belonged to the Adawite minority... Deadly Clashes erupted between security forces and gunmen loyal to Bashar Al-Assad, leading to nearly 1500 deaths in just two days."[14]

14. In his latest social media post, Trump issued a "last warning" "to **Hamas** to release all remaining hostages, ... He also told the people of **Gaza** that "a beautiful future awaits" them but not if the hostages aren't released." But in essence, Trump does not deflect from his stance to depart, permanently, the entire Palestinian population of Gaza to an as yet unknown location. The White House recently reconfirmed this and rejected an alternative proposal for rebuilding Gaza put forth by Arab nations ... He first announced his plan in front of Netanyahu on Feb. 4. It all started back then with: "we will own it." Later, in the press conference held with King Abdullah II of Jordon in the Oval Office, it sounded like "we are not going to buy it, we are going to have it, we are going to keep it, we will cherish it."[15] Why Trump Doubling Down on deporting Palestinians from the Strip? Perhaps because he and Netanyahu want to erase evidence of genocide, writes a West Asia Scholar.
15. "US president Trump said on Friday that he was "strongly considering" imposing sanctions and tariffs on Russia until a ceasefire and permanent peace deal is reached in its war against Ukraine."[16]
16. "US to use AI to revoke visas of international students it perceives support Hamas......"[17]
17. "President Donald Trump has virtually shuttered USAID, his country's aid agency. He says it was a morass of waste and corruption, enabling sundry corrupt dictators to rip off the US." ..... He has already pulled out of the World Health Organization and Paris Agreement on climate change ..... He does not on appear to believe in global cooperation ..... The US once positioned itself, warts and all, as the benevolent hegemon of the 20th Century. The rules – oriented economic order it created brought about unprecedented global GDP growth and prosperity. But Trump has decided that benevolence is a mug's game and bullying works for better ...... "Of the three, World Bank, IMF and IDA (which depends on cash contri-butions from richer countries every three years so) "Given Trump's rhetoric, he looks certain to pull out of the IDA....... But...... he is more likely he stick with the Bank and IMF."[18]

The above are some of the current news, announcements by eminent political leaders, inferences of scholars of different nations, web sites, headlines, etc., appeared in news paper like Time of India, New Delhi, India and, Bangkok Post, Thailand for perusal of the readers of this Study. Similar types or with little bit of differences in words/phrases could be added in innumerable counts from variegated social media till the time frame counting upto the date of the publication of this study. But all these lead us to conclude one irrevocable truth. Becoming uncivilized let us frankly say that **there is found lack of real trust among different nations of the world** which has resulted into repudiation of all the desired impact of ethical, human values and conduct based behaviour. To put it differently, **the model of global education & training is yet to fumble the group of people for whom it has been recommended.** The phrases like loves and **compassion, Non-violence, righteousness, discipline, cognitive, emotional and nuro-science rules etc. are yet to secure the attention of strong political and administrative leaders of the world.**

Anyhow we have suggested the best we could; three **Progressive Sustainable Development Goals**, were – not added to PSDG17 described earlier, as the same are altogether innovative in their contents, on the one hand and are closely connected with the obtained current scenario as well with the completely hypothetical time frame beyond Mid-Twenty Second century i.e., beyond 2150/ 2175 and onward. First Two PSDG:18 and PSDG:19 are portrayed hereunder and the last one (PSDG20) in the concluding Chapter on: 'Epilogue'.

PSDG:18 'NO MORE WORLD WARS & ARMED CONFLICTS/ DISPUTES/PROGRESSIVE SUSTAINABLE DEVELOPMENT GOAL: 18

As and when any strong political leader/Group says, that we will not allow the Third World War to happen, it indirectly means, that there exist a possibility of having Third World War in the world. Likewise, when different countries buy weapons of different kinds, it implies that there exist the possibility of using these weapons. Otherwise, why should any country buy weapons and incur heavy expenditure. In the light of growing situation on both of these fronts, it is proposed that the new **PSDG:18** on **'NO MORE WORLD WARS/ARMED CONFLICTS & NUCLEAR WEAPONS ZERO – IN PROCESS** be persued by World Union of Visionary Nations with the target of **Eliminating World Wars, Armed Conflicts, and Nuclear Weapons** with a view to achieve a state of peace and eliminating the threat of nuclear weapons, with the specific goal of **Zero Armed Conflicts and nuclear weapons in process.** There are 3 broad rationale of implementing this PSDG: 18:

(i) **Humanitarian Impact:** Armed conflicts and nuclear weapons pose and existential threat to humanity, causing immense human suffering, displacement, and loss of life.

(ii) **Developmental Impact:** Armed conflicts and nuclear weapons divert resources away from progressive sustainable development hindering acceleration of growth.

(iii) **Global Security:** Eliminating nuclear weapons and armed conflicts is essential for global security, stability and peace.

Indicator may be set for measuring success in terms of reducing the armed conflicts, number of countries having nuclear weapons programmers and global military expenditure. Zero-in process about Nuclear Weapons world not only need the thorough study of official documents, but also those brought out by Research Institutions, Think Tanks, Federations Constituted by different countries of the world including News Organizations and Media outlets, Academic Journals like Journal of Nuclear Materials, Nonproliferation Review International Security and online Databases (Nuclear Threat Initiative (NTI), Global Security Organization and World Nuclear Association). In the context, it may be added that different Key words are used in varied sources such as "Nuclear-Weopons Production" "Nuclear Proliferation", "Nuclear Disarmament", and **Country specific Nuclear Programs,** e.g. **"North Korea Nuclear Programme."**

The **Potential means** of implementing this PSDG:18 are:

(1) **Strengthening International Diplomacy;**

(2) Disarmaments and non-proliferation treats, such as the **Treaty on the Non-proliferation of Nuclear Weapons (NPT);**

(3) **Supporting conflict prevention** and resolution mechanisms, such as mediation, arbitration, and peacekeeping; and,

(4) Promoting global education and awareness about the devasting effects of armed conflicts and nuclear weapons.

PSDG:19: ENSURING REGULATORY FRAMEWORKS FOR RESPONSIBLE AI PROGRESSIVE SUSTAINABLE DEVELOPMENT GOAL: 19[19]

AI (Artificial Intelligence) is advancing rapidly transforming numerous industries and aspects of our lives concerning Healthcare, Education, Finance, Transportation, Cybersecurity, Job market etc. However, it's unlikely to completely replace human beings due to its numerous limitations like creativity and imagination, emotional intelligence, complexity of decision-making, and their contextual understanding. Even so, the fact remains that we are living in an AI – driven world which in desirable too within a carefully developed **'Regulatory Framework-'**. The reason is obvious. There are researchers and experts who firmly believe that AI has the potential to surpass human intelligence and potentially replace humans in various domains.

ELON MUSK, for example, has expressed concerns about the potential risks of advanced AI, stating that it could be humanity's **"biggest existential threat". NICK BOSTRON,** a philosopher and Director of the **Future of Humanity Institute,** has argued that advanced AI could pose an extential risk to humanity. And **STEPHEN HAWKING,** just prior to his passing, warned the world that the development of **AI could spell the end of human race.** Even though, the world is on perpetual debate as to what and when shall turn out to be the reality, it is persuasively redolent to adopt this additional PSDG:19 to begin with upto

Mid-twenty Two Century (2250), subject to enhancement of its execution for an infinite time frame or till its (AI) is substituted by some more enriching development.

TARGET PROPOSED

Accordingly, we should establish and implement regulatory frameworks to ensure the developments, and use of artificial Intelligence (AI) in a transparent, accountable, and with human values.

RATIONALE

- **Ethical Concerns:** AI development raises ethical concerns, such as bias, privacy, and job displacement which require regulatory oversight.
- **Social Impact;** AI has significant social implications, and regulatory frameworks can ensure that AI benefits Society as a whole.
- **Innovation:** Regulatory Frameworks can also foster innovation by providing clarity and certainty for AI developers.
- **Potential Indicators:** For ensuring that it is happening could include:
    (1) **Number of Countries** with AI specific regulatory framework;
    (2) **Proportion of AI Systems** with built-in transparency and accountability mechanisms;
    (3) **Number of AI** – related ethical incidents reported: Decrease in number of AI – Related ethical incidents;
    (4) **Proportion of AI** – developers that adhere to responsible AI development principles; and
    (5) **Level of public trust in AI systems. And, potential Means** of implementation could be:
        (i) **Establishing regulatory frameworks** that address AI-specific challenges and opportunities;
        (ii) **Promoting transparency and accountability** in AI-development and deployment;
        (iii) **Foster International cooperation** to develop and implement consistent regulatory frameworks for AI;
        (iv) **Educating the public and policymakers,** and AI developers about the benefits and risks of AI; and
        (v) **Promoting responsible AI development** practices, such as fairness, transparency and accountability.

Having discussed as many as 19 PSDGs, let us add our synoptic ultimate outcome. Undisputedly each one of them plays an important role in elevation of progressive sustainable development in larger or less manner but of all the PSDG pertaining to promotion of **CAPRICIOUS GLOBAL EDUCATION** is of paramount importance. It it's done life long for human beings of different countries of the world sincerely then the causes that disturbs global peace and growth would themselves stand **'DESTROYED'.** It is, however, not to suggest that other PSDGs be neglected or ignored or not established. The vivacious and invigorative be animated on **GLOBAL EDUCATION FOR ALL PERSONS INCLUDING BUT NOT LIMITED TO STUDENTS, WORKING PROFESSIONAL, ADMISNISTRATORS, POLITICIANS AND INDIVIDUALS FROM ALL SOCIO-ECONOMIC BACKGROUNDS, GENDERS, AND AGE GROUPS EXCEPTING THE INCAPACIATED & INFANTS.**

ANNEXTURE ON: PSDG: 19 "ON ENSURING REGULATORY FRAMEWORKS FOR RESPONSIBLE AI PROGRESSIVE SUSTAINABLE DEVELOPMENT GOAL: 19"

I. CORE PRINCIPLES

1. Human – centric AI.
2. Transparency and Explainability.
3. Accountability and Responsibility.
4. Privacy and Data Protection.
5. Security and Cybersecurity.
6. Sustainability and Environmental Responsibility.
7. Inclusivity and Diversity.
8. International Cooperation.

II. DEVELOPMENT PILLARS

1. Research and Innovation.
2. Education and Training.
3. Infrastructure and Deployment.
4. Ethics and Governance.
5. International Cooperation.

III. CONTROL MECHANISMS: GLOBAL AI REGULATION FRAMEWORK COMPONENTS

1. AI Standards and Certification.
2. AI Ethics Board.
3. AI Regulatory Agency.
4. AI Incident Response Team.
5. AI Audit and Evaluation.

IV. KEY REGULATIONS

1. Data Protection and Privacy.
2. AI Safety and Security.
3. AI Bias and Fairness.
4. AI Transparency and Explainability.
5. AI Accountability and Responsibility.

V. IMPLEMENTATION ROADMAP

A. Short term (0-5 years)

1. Establish WUVN-ERF R-AI: SPSDG: 19.
2. Develop AI Standards and Certification.
3. Create AI Ethics Board and Regulatory Agency.
4. Implement AI Incident Response Team.

B. Medium term (6-10 years)

1. Develop AI Education and Training Programmes.
2. Establish AI Infrastructure and Deployment Guidelines.
3. Implement AI Audit and Evaluation Frameworks.
4. Enhance international collaboration and cooperation.

C. Long term (10-20 years)

1. Achieve Global AI Standards and Certification.
2. Establish AI Governance and Regulation Framework.
3. Ensure AI safety, security and accountability.
4. Foster global AI innovation and development.

VI. GLOBAL AI GOVERNANCE STRUCTURE

1. World Union of Visionary Nations-AI Commission (WUVN-AI-C).
2. AI Governance Board.
3. AI Regulatory Agency.
4. AI Ethics Committee.
5. AI Incident Response Team.

VII. INTERNATIONAL COOPERATION

1. Multilateral Agreements and Treaties.
2. Bilateral Cooperation and Partnerships.
3. International AI Research Collaborations.
4. Global AI Standards and Certification.

VIII. TECHNOLOGICAL INTEGRATION

1. Blockchain-based AI Governance.
2. AI-Powered Monitoring and Evaluation.
3. Cybersecurity Measures.
4. Data-driven Decision-Making.

IX. EDUCATION AND CAPACITY BUILDING

1. AI Literacy Programs.
2. AI Education and Training.
3. AI Research and Development Capacity Building.
4. AI Policy and Governance Capacity Building.

X. MONITORING AND EVALUATION

1. Regular Performance Assessments.
2. AI Incident Reporting and Response.
3. AI Audit and Evaluation Framework.
4. Continuous Improvement and Adaptation.

ENDNOTES

1. The Times of India, News Paper, India, March 18, 2025.
2. Ibid, March 16, 2025, p. 1.
3. The Economic Times, New Delhi, India, 17th March, 20025, p. 3.
4. The Times of India, New Delhi, India, March 19, 2025 p. 18.
5. Ibid., p. 18.
6. Ibid., p. 20.
7. The Economic Times, New Delhi/Gurgaon, India, 13 March 2025, p. 6.
8. Times of India, New Delhi, India, 11 March, 2025.
9. India's Foreign Minister, Shri S. Jaishankar quoted from the Times of India, News Paper, New Delhi, India, March 7, 2025, p. 1.
10. The Times of India, New Delhi, Newspaper, India, March 6, 2025, p. 2.
11. All the quoted material is owned to Maria Fernanda Espinosa, a former President of the UN General Assembly, is Executive Director of GWL VOICES for a Green and Inclusive Recovery Project. She was a Member of the COP29 International Advisory Committee, Bangkok Post, Thailand, December 13, 2024, p. 8.
12. Bangkok Post, Newspaper, Thailand. December 9, 2025.
13. Twitter/MEAgov., March 6, 2005.
14. Times of India, News Paper, New Delhi, India, March 10, 2025, p. 23 and Times of India Video, March, 11, 2025.
15. Times of India, New paper, New Delhi, India March 7, 2025, p. 1.
16. Times of India, Newspaper, New Delhi, India, March 8, 2025, p. 2.
17. Ibid.
18. Times of India, Newspaper, New Delhi, India, March 9, 2025, p. 22.
19. The details of $PSDG_{19}$ can be perused in Annexure on PSDG: 19 ON "ENSURING REGULATORY FRAMEWORKS FOR RESPONSIBLE AI PROGRESSIVE SUSTAINABLE DEVELOPMENT GOAL: 19" given in this Chapter at its end.

CHAPTER - 12

EPILOGUE: VISUALIZING THE ROADMAP FOR HUMAN PROGRESS BEYOND CENTURY 35 (3500 +)[1]

To close this Study, we further propose to briefly highlight the prominent developments this world beyond the Mid-Twenty Second century (2150-2175) way the World Union of Visionary Nations should deal with them, though most of the period spanning beyond 2150 would be slightly hypothetical as against fully hypothetical. In order to cover up this span of timeframe, we propose to have another PSDG20 by the World Union of Visionary Nations. For the sake of convenience it may be phrased as "**Progressively Sustainable Development Goal: 20 on HUMAN PROGRESS BEYOND MID Twenty SECOND CENTURY TILL CENTURY THIRTY FIFTH & BEYOND**".

Century-wise, WU of VNs could take up the under detailed tasks for the foundations for a sustainable future for human beings:

1. **Century 21-23 (2150-2300):**
   - (i) Attempt to achieve 100% **Renewable Energy,** phasing out fossil fuels.
   - (ii) **Develop and deploy carbon capture, utilization and storage technologies** to reverse climate change.
   - (iii) **Implementing regenerative agriculture** practices, reducing synthetic fertilizers and pesticides, and promoting bio-diversity.
   - (iv) **Establishing a robust, inclusive and effective global governance system** to address shared challenges.
   - (v) **Life long learning** in contents and applications of Global Education and Training.

2. **Century 24-25 [2301-2500]:** These two centuries must be focused on the **Human Well-being and Flourishing.** Accordingly, the WU of VNs should attempt to:
   - (i) Achieve universal access to **quality healthcare, eradicating infectius diseases and promoting mental well-being.**
   - (ii) **Progressively sustainable urban planning** in order to prioritize green spaces, clean energy, and social cohesion.
   - (iii) **Implementation of a global basic income guarantees,** ensuring economic security and dignity for all.
   - (iv) Launch **a global effort to restore degraded ecosystems;** preserving biodiversity and promoting ecological balance.
   - (v) **Fostering global citizenship,** cultural exchange, and empathy, promoting a sense of shared humanity.
3. **Century 26-27 (2501-2700):** During these two centuries the emphasis may be on **'Technological Advancements'** and **'Space Exploration'.**[2] As such, the efforts may be put in on:
   - (i) **Developing and integrating AI** and automation technologies for augmenting human capabilities, ensuring equitable benefits.
   - (ii) **Space Exploration and Colonization.** As such the understanding of the universe may be deepened and **sustainable human settlements on the Moon, Mars, and beyond be ensured.**[3]
   - (iii) **Innovative Materials and Manufacturing Technologies** be developed in order to facilitate development of new products and sustainable infrastructure.
   - (iv) Harnessing the power of **quantum computing** while ensuring robust cybersecurity measures to protect **global digital infrastructure.**
   - (v) **Establishing Communication Channels with other intelligent life forms,** fostering interstellar cooperation and mutual understanding.
4. **CENTURY 28-29 [2701-2900]:** These two centuries are likely to be more hypothetical vis-à-vis 26 and 27th centuries. Hence greater emphasis is likely to be on **'Human Evolution and Transcendence.** The efforts would be concentrated on:
   - (i) **Achieving significant Advancements in Life Extension**

and Regenerative Medicines, enhancing human healthspan and quality of life.

(ii) **Exploring the potential of merging human** and artificial intelligence, redefining human identity and capabilities.

(iii) **Transcending Planetary Boundaries:** Developing technologies to transcend planetary boundaries, enabling humanity to thrive in space and explore the cosmos.

(iv) **Fostering a sense of cosmic citizenship,** promoting responsible stewardship of the universe and its resources.

(v) **Developing Strategies to Mitigate Existential Risks,** ensuring humanity's long term – survival and prosperity.

5. **Century 30-31 [3001-3100]:** We may call it **GALACTIC CIVILIZATION.** The tasks that would be included are:

   (i) Establishing a **network of settlements** across the galaxy.

   (ii) **Developing and deploying Advanced Propulsion Systems,** enabling faster – than – light travel and deeper exploration of the Cosmos.

   (iii) **Establishing a Galactic Government** or coalition, promoting cooperation, peace and sustainable development among planetary civilizations.

   (iv) **Developing and Implementing sustainable practices** for managing Cosmic resources, such as asteroid mining and energy harvesting.

   (v) **Implementing post-scarcity economics,** ensuring that advanced technologies provide abundant resources and energy for all.

6. **Century 32-33 (3201-3300): Could be phrased as 'Transcendence and Evolution'** Century. In this century efforts would be done for:

   (i) **Achieving a Seamless merging between human and artificial intelligence,** redefining human identity and capabilities.

   (ii) **Developing Technologies** to achieve infinite life extension and regeneration, enabling humans to transcend mortality.

   (iii) **Exploring the frontiers of transhumanism and Posthumanism,** evolving humans to evolve into new forms of life.

(iv) **Develop technologies to enhance human consciousness and awareness, enabling deeper connections with the cosmos and other forms of life.**

(v) **Developing Strategies to Mitigate Existential Risks,** ensuring humanity's long term survival and prosperity.

7. **Century 34-35 [3401-3500]: We may also call it as a century of 'Multiverse Exploration'**

 (i) **Developing and Testing Theories of the Multiverse,** enabling humanity to explore and understand the vast expanse of the cosmos.

 (ii) **Developing and deploying wormhole technology,** ennobling faster-than-light travel between universes and dimensions.

 (iii) **Establishing relationships with other intelligent life forms** across the multiverse, promoting cooperation, peace, and sustainable development.

 (iv) **Developing and implementing sustainable practices for managing Cosmic energy and resources across the multiverse.**

 (v) **Establishing a framework for governance and ethics** in the multiverse, ensuring responsible exploration and development.

8. **Beyond Century 35 (3501+):** It can also be termed as a century of **'Cosmic Horizon'.** The prime focus points in **Century Beyond 3501+** would be on:

 (i) **Cosmic Evolution and Transformation** i.e., we would continue to evolve and transform humanity, enabling us to transcend our current limitations and explore the vast expanse of the Cosmos.

 (ii) **Multiverse Citizenship and Stewardship** – Fostering a sense of multiverse citizenship and stewardship, promoting responsible exploration and development of the Cosmos.

 (iii) **Developing strategies to mitigate existential risks** and ensuring humanity's longterm survival and prosperity in the multiverse.

 (iv) **Continue to develop technologies to enhance human consciousness and awareness,** enabling deeper connections with the cosmos and other forms of life.

(v) **The Cosmic Horizon:** Exploring the frontiers of the Cosmos, pushing the boundaries of human knowledge and understanding.

The above **PSDG:20** thus offer a meagre (say broadly upto 2500), and high level hypothetical (say thereafter 2501-3500+) roadmap for an human progress, spanning multiple centuries and exploring the frontiers of cosmos. What would happen actually, and how it would be tackled in real life situations, is simply a matter to be seen. **We have genuinely attempted to make this study catholic and befitting to both the foreseeable unhypothetical as well meager to highly hypothetical timeframes.** If some turn down to the extent of ill-boding existential to human being happens-well none can rule out. But it will not happen with if the PSDG:20 is kept alive **genuflection by World Union of Visionary Nations.**

ENDNOTES

1. In an article "Earth Waming at its Fastest pace in 10,000 years- business leaders must heed the Anthropocene', appeared in the Economic Times, New Delhi Gurgaon, India, 13 March 2025, p. 1, are quite relevant to the 'Epilogue'. These in brief are as under:

   (i) In 2023 with industrial emission rising, Earth's glaciers lost a huge **600 gigatons of water** this impacts many species. This is the largest annual loss ever recorded.

   (ii) Cities of the Future? As ice caps melt in the Arctic and Antarc the world's seas have risen twice as fast in the last 30 years.

   (iii) Since 1750, human activities, from agriculture to industry, have released **1.5 Trillion tons of carbon dioxide into the atmosphere.**

   (iv) **Surface Temperature** has increased by 1.17° Celsius over just the last Century.

   (v) **Oceans have warmed by 1.45° Celsius** – this has made sea levels rise twice as fast in the last three decades.

   (vi) **Antarctica is losing 150 billion tons** of ice mass per year.

   (vii) **Arctic Ice** is **Shrinking at 12.2% per decade.**

   (viii) Since 1975, **70% of Earth's wildlife has been lost due to human Impacts like deforestation.**

2. We are today **not even during Mid Twenty First Century** (2050-2075), yet, we find the Report on landing of Sunita Williams and Butch Wilmore, NASA astronauts in the Times of India, 19th March, 2025 (Indian News Paper, New Delhi/Gurgaon). It reads as thus:

   "NASA astronauts Sunita Williams and Butch Wilmore made their return to Earth after an extended nine-month stay abroad the International Space

Station (ISS). Initially slated for just eight days, their mission was extended due to technical issues with the Boing Starliner spacecraft.

Also please read the article appeared in the Times of India, News Paper, New Delhi, March, 20, 2025 at page 20, by Chethan Kumar titled "What Suni & Every other Astronaut Endure up There"; it briefly describe the primary challenges faced when travelling to space; how does weightlessness impact the human body; what are the psychological challenges of staying in space; how does the absence of Earth's atmosphere affect astronauts' health; how are food, water, and waste managed in space; how are tech advancements helping astronauts stay longer in space; and, how do astronauts prepare for these challenges.

3. In the context of Space Exploration, it would be of interest to note that Elan Musk has founded Space X as a private aerospace manufacturer and Space Transport Services Company in 2002 with the primary goal to reduce space transportation costs and enable the colonization of Mars. It's Future Plans are:
   (i) Establishing a permanent human presence on Mars; and
   (ii) Plans to send private missions to the Moon, including tourist trips and scientific expeditions; the Times of India; New Paper, New Delhi/Gurgaon, 19 March 2025; Space X's Starship Progress.